Rising
Hope

Rising Hope

RECIPES & STORIES
FROM LUMINARY BAKERY

Written by Rachel Stonehouse & Kaila H. Johnson

With Alice Williams & Rachael Coulson

LUMINARY BAKERY

HQ

CONTENTS

INTRODUCTION

BY ALICE WILLIAMS,
FOUNDER OF LUMINARY BAKERY

If you were to walk into a Luminary Bakery on an ordinary day, you would be met with the smell of freshly baked cinnamon swirls, and a warm greeting from one of our café team. You would see a mix of locals gathering for a quiet coffee or holding a meeting, the hustle and bustle of cakes being decorated, and you might see several women coming in and being greeted like family.

Luminary is a London-based bakery on a mission to empower some of the UK's most disadvantaged women. In this book, you are invited behind the scenes, to learn our treasured recipes and hear the stories of hope that rise behind our bakery doors.

Over the years, we have often been asked to write a recipe book, with loyal customers longing to know the secret to our cinnamon swirls or fluffy focaccia. And many of the women we have supported through baking have been keen to share their life stories, to encourage others to find hope in any circumstances. We have met so many courageous women, and working with them to create this book has given us all the opportunity to reflect on how far we have come as individuals, as well as collectively.

Meeting women who were experiencing extreme poverty, disadvantage and violence was the inspiration for starting Luminary. There was one encounter in particular that stands out in my mind...

I remember where I was when I met her, standing on Vallance Road near Whitechapel at one o'clock in the morning, with the City of London skyline behind us. I was volunteering with a local charity, Door of Hope, taking out necessary supplies to women working in the red-light area. She was cold, fed up and not making enough money. When I asked if there were any other ways for her to earn an income, she replied, 'I don't know how to do anything else, I've been doing this since I was thirteen.'

I met many women like her and not just those 'street-working'; I also volunteered in a homeless hostel, many of whose female residents had experienced abuse and were living in poverty. The world of skyscrapers, wealth, high-end restaurants and coffee chains – just a stone's throw away from where they were living – could have been a million miles away for the lack of opportunities it offered them. All had lived through harrowing things and yet they were survivors, fighters, hustlers, mothers, defenders – these women had potential. I couldn't stand by and see it go to waste. I couldn't bear to see them struggling to get by every day, questioning their value, and unable to provide a different future for their children.

Although we didn't have much, our small team from a local church (Kahaila on Brick Lane) decided to set about changing the landscape for these local women forever. Abigail Mifsud (a food blogger and home baker), Sarah Harrison (also a home baker and a volunteer chef in the homeless hostel) and I decided to use the skills our team had and began to teach the women we met how to bake.

Initially, this was just for women in the homeless hostel, which was a great setting for us to start getting to know local women. Each of them had a different journey that had led them there: some had fled a violent partner; some had left prison and had nowhere to go; some had been rough sleeping and this was finally a place to call home. Some of the women were already great cooks and some had never tried baking before, but they all wanted the opportunity to do something creative, something for themselves, and something they could share with others. Their skills began to improve and we spent time investing in them as individuals, in their personal growth, overcoming trauma and preparing to build a career in the food industry.

And hope began to rise.

Generously, we were given space in the kitchen of another local church to bake products to sell at Kahaila Café, and we took samples to other local companies. Our little business gained momentum and we secured a contract with Ben and Jerry's to provide all the baked goods for their first UK store. We soon outgrew the church kitchen and had the opportunity to move into a larger kitchen nearby. Here, we brought in even more women to train.

The first day of our training course is always nerve-wracking for trainees as they take the brave step to enter

RISING HOPE

a new environment and open themselves up to the support of both the Luminary team and their fellow trainees. Baking can feel intimidating for some – perhaps you have a hint of that same trepidation opening this book for the first time. But at Luminary, baking is for everyone. One baking session stands out in my memory, when a woman who struggled with her concentration and comprehension of theory eventually saw her loaf of bread come out of the oven. She burst into tears and exclaimed, 'I can't have made that! It's so perfect!' When we finally convinced her that it was in fact her loaf, her confidence soared.

We start with the basics, as our trainees venture into the world of baking and begin to understand the importance of thoroughly reading a recipe before enthusiastically launching in. Then, we gradually build on their accomplishments, challenging them with more technical bakes as their skills and confidence grow. You are welcome to take a similar approach, challenging yourself to try a new product weekly, as our women do, or simply dip into the book to try out a new recipe when you fancy, or have an occasion to bake for.

The support we offer women at Luminary is not just centred around baking – we also want women to learn, to dream and to share with one another. Seeing them start to take brave steps in opening up is magical. As Brené Brown says, 'We can't be brave in the big world without at least one small safe space to work through our fears and falls.' This is the space Luminary has always sought to be. There is no judgement here – about your past, present or your future.

As Luminary has grown, we have built strong partnerships with organisations who support women with traumatic life experiences. They might have survived human trafficking, domestic abuse, the criminal justice system, or leaving care. Often, the common factors that they have each lived through are poverty, homelessness and mental health issues as a result of the trauma they have endured. Some services classify women who have experienced this type of multiple disadvantage as 'vulnerable' adults, and while it is important to recognise where people need extra support, in our experience women shouldn't necessarily be labelled as vulnerable. After all, it is their strength and resilience that has got them to where they are today. At Luminary, we have moved towards the word 'disadvantaged'. This makes it clear that the women's life experiences are down to their situation, and not a comment on their strength of character.

One of our favourite moments every year is the graduation ceremony that we hold to celebrate our women completing the full six-month programme. At this, they display their show-stopping cakes and we present them with their certificates. Our first group of trainees graduated in March 2015, at one of the most powerful and emotional evenings I've ever experienced. They invited friends and family, showcased their impressive bakes, shared a little of their stories, and we celebrated them. They deserved it. These women, and the many others who have graduated since – the women in this book – are now making their way in the world, building their careers and inspiring us every day.

Luminary Bakery found its very own home in 2016, on Allen Road in Stoke Newington, after two years of baking in generous kitchens nearby. It had always been our dream to move from wholesale production to opening our doors to the public, creating more job opportunities for the women we train. And with the help of significant grants and a crowdfunding campaign to buy equipment, this vision became a reality. Our fourth cohort started their training the day after we moved in; needless to say, it was chaos!

But we soon found our feet, and those women were so excited to be the first to benefit from the new space.

Over the last few years, Luminary has gone from strength to strength – growing our social enterprise into something sustainable, opening a second location in Camden, training nearly 100 women, tackling huge orders with a small team and getting to the point where we were even making cakes for The Duchess of Sussex! All the while, we have journeyed with our women through starting their careers, building their own businesses, moving house, getting married, overcoming their fears, navigating the complicated transition from welfare to work, raising children, and even being by their side during childbirth.

This is the Luminary family.

Too often, violence and trauma isolate us from community, when that is the very thing we need the most. We want to thank every woman who has joined Luminary, because it takes courage to step into the bakery on that first day. We hope that they have felt welcomed, accepted, loved and inspired, and we know that they have helped create that safe haven for others, too. These women are why Luminary exists, and they make it an exciting, uplifting and vibrant community to be a part of. This book is a chance for them – and for others who have been involved – to share some of their stories with you, along with their favourite recipes.

This is a book bursting with hope – filled with the stories of women who held on to hope when they thought all was lost. Each narrative is uniquely powerful, but together they remind us that strength comes in community.

Every woman has shown immense courage to survive her circumstances alone, but it is only when she is embraced by others that she can really start to fulfil her potential. There are caring friends, compassionate doctors and pro-active support workers who have all given these women the confidence to take brave steps in their lives and careers.

Baking is special and it connects people in a way that is difficult to describe. Baking together bridges cultures, social classes and differing life experiences. Baking can raise hope in people who had forgotten their own potential, their power.

Our dream for this book is that it inspires you to raise hope in your community, too. Maybe you will bake one of these recipes to share with someone who is going through a tough time. Perhaps you will be as brave as the women in this book to share with others your journey of overcoming adversity. You might challenge a friend to bake through the book with you and go on a journey of discovering your potential. Whatever way this inspires you, we thank you for joining in with the hope that is rising at Luminary.

HALIMOT'S STORY

Halimot's story truly represents the rising hope that is always within us, even in the darkest of times, and we're so proud to call her one of Luminary's graduates.

At a young age, Halimot was trafficked into modern slavery by someone she trusted. Although she eventually escaped after several years of being held against her will, the trauma of her experience dramatically impacted her day-to-day living. Years later, after overcoming so much and starting a family, she continued to keep her past a secret out of concern for her children and worry that the traffickers would find her again.

It wasn't until Halimot's depression spiralled out of control, that she finally opened up to her doctor about her past. This was the moment when things began to change. She was introduced to a charity that worked with women from trafficked backgrounds, offering support and counselling. It was then that the charity introduced her to Alice and Luminary Bakery.

'I didn't trust people at all – I lost trust completely – but I thought I'd give Luminary a chance. On the first day, sharing it with people who understood my background, I knew I was going to do it! The care I received from the ladies at Luminary brought up so many emotions. Someone even offered me a drink! It had been a long time since someone cared for me like that.'

At the start, each day was a challenge to overcome, as things didn't always work out as she wanted them to. But, unlike before, she had people to fall back on and Halimot found the encouragement she received from Luminary therapeutic. As she began to grow in her knowledge of baking, each day became a success. Not only did Halimot graduate from our programme, but she went on to start her own business (see page 255).

Halimot's love of food and of bringing people together has grown into an innate desire to create community, whether at her children's school, in her neighbourhood or at Luminary events. Her former life, where isolation became the only option, has slowly transitioned into a life with rising hope in others, full of encouragement, strength and love for people.

'Whenever people say that my baking tastes good, it heals me! I don't see my clients as simply people ordering from me, I see them as helping me process and heal.'

Halimot continues to bring a warmth to Luminary that impacts each new group of trainees. Together, she has been part of helping us build a family of warriors and overcomers, leaning on and encouraging each other, and empowering each woman that comes through our doors to reach their potential. We are a family! Through celebrations, heartache, business challenges, and the ups and downs of life, we work through it all together. Halimot's wisdom, advice and encouragement never ceases to amaze us – she is an incredibly gifted woman.

'Never give up! What has happened in the past has happened. You cannot change the clock. Don't give up, but change it in a positive way. There's no going back to yesterday. There's only moving forward to tomorrow!'

Now, *that* is rising hope.

EQUIPMENT & BAKING NOTES

We recognise that no one has everything – whether that's specific tools, access to certain ingredients, financial resources, or even time; we're all short of something! With this in mind, we've included bakes that cover a range of different options. There are recipes for when you're short of time (which take about 30 minutes to make); economical recipes (cheap to make or which make use of food that would normally be thrown away); and recipes for those with special dietary requirements (vegan, gluten-free and lactose-free). The Special Indexes section on page 250 will help you find them.

Measurements: As bakers, we're passionate about precise measurements and weighing out ingredients accurately. A recipe is a specific set of instructions and, if followed faithfully, should produce consistent bakes the way the author intended. Unlike a soup, where a few extra vegetables, stock or seasoning could go undetected, where baking is concerned even a little deviation from the recipe can have a big effect!

We find using grams to measure ingredients (rather than volume measurements) produces more consistent products. For this reason, in our bakery we always use electronic scales to measure ingredients. We weigh everything from salt to flour, bananas to oil.

Electronic scales are more accurate than mechanical ones because they are more sensitive, allowing us to measure small incremental amounts of ingredients as well as liquids straight into our mixing bowls.

You only need to become familiar with the 'tare' function on electronic scales, which will bring the read-out back to zero after you have placed your bowl on the scales. This saves on washing up (always a bonus), but is also far easier and quicker than trying to judge the level of water in a jug or to guestimate 11g of salt, for instance. Fruit, vegetables and herbs also vary in size depending on the variety and supplier, so for these too we give a weight in grams to ensure a consistent bake.

We have given liquid quantities in ml, but if you have electronic scales it's much more accurate to measure liquids by weight, rather than doing it by eye. Wonderfully, 1ml of water weighs 1g, so it's an easy conversion.

Similarly, for baking, don't use any old household teaspoons and tablespoons to measure out your ingredients, as they can vary in size. Instead, use a set of measuring spoons. All teaspoon and tablespoon measurements are level unless stated otherwise.
1 tsp = 5ml
1 tbsp = 15ml

Ovens: Just like people, every oven has a different temperament, running at different temperatures to what they're supposed to be programmed to. This can sadly result in over- or under-cooked bakes and be so disappointing if you've just invested time and money into creating a recipe. If you bake regularly, you hopefully have a good grasp on whether (and if so, where) your oven has hotspots and whether it bakes hotter or cooler than other ovens. We advise you to adjust the temperatures in the recipes slightly to account for this and also rotate products within the oven to help give them an even bake. If you're new to your oven, we recommend using an oven thermometer, which will reveal the true temperature of your oven. You can then adjust the oven dial to achieve the temperature required in each recipe.

Scales: As we've just mentioned, if you bake regularly and have the means to invest in a set of electronic (digital) scales, we can't recommend them enough – they will transform your baking! But if not, don't fear – we've made sure all the recipes in this book can be made with whatever equipment you have, and very small precise measurements (such as 11g of salt) are also given in teaspoons for ease.

Electric stand or hand mixers: Many of our recipes require an electric stand or hand mixer – but if you don't own one, don't worry! We ran our first three training courses teaching our trainees to make everything by hand. For creaming or beating mixtures together, use a wooden spoon or a firm spatula. And for anything that needs to be whisked, a wire balloon whisk works just as well. It will just take a little longer and require a bit more elbow grease!

Bench scrapers: Lots of bakers use a simple piece of equipment called a 'bench scraper' for making bread or decorating cakes. It's a rectangle of plastic or metal, usually with one curved and one straight edge, used to divide doughs, scrape them off surfaces and help knead. When kneading bread, it can be tempting to dust the work surface you're using with flour to stop the dough sticking, but this can result in a dryer, harder bread, because you end up mixing all that extra flour into the dough. Instead, fearlessly let the dough stick to the surface and use a bench scraper to scrape off any that's stuck, bringing it back into the ball of dough. A bench scraper can also be used as a cake scraper, to evenly smooth icing over the surface of a layer cake. If you're making lots of bread, particularly very wet doughs such as focaccia, you might find investing a few quid in one makes a world of difference.

Cake decorating tools: At Luminary, we use a few bits of equipment only keen cake makers usually own, such as a turntable, palette knife and cake scraper. They make getting a perfectly smooth finish on a cake a lot easier and are well worth the investment if you decorate cakes regularly. If you don't have these to hand, you can place the cake on a large, flat plate and rotate it on your work surface instead of using a turntable. And a butter knife and spatula are sufficient in place of a palette knife or cake scraper.

Silicone spatula: We always have a silicone spatula on hand, for getting every last bit of mixture out of the bowl or saucepan.

Pastry brush: You'll find a pastry brush very useful for glazing and greasing, too.

Baking paper and silicone baking mats/tin liners: There is sometimes confusion over whether to use baking paper (sometimes called baking parchment) or greaseproof paper. Greaseproof paper is better for sandwich wrapping as a lot of baked goods will stick like glue to it. If you're standing perplexed in the supermarket, opt to buy 'baking paper', which is the better option. For baking cookies, silicone baking mats can be a useful and sustainable purchase to replace baking paper, as they can be washed up and re-used many times. You can now also buy re-usable silicone cake tin liners.

BREAD

There is something inviting about the smell of freshly baked bread. The delicious warm fragrance brings to mind moments, whether dreamed or experienced, of the comforts of home, when families gather and food is shared. In our Luminary cafés, the aromas from the bakery fill each room, awakening nostalgia and the anticipation of flavours before you get the chance to satisfy your mouthwatering cravings.

Through learning to make our signature cinnamon swirls and fluffy focaccia, Luminary trainees have found breadmaking to be therapeutic – it brings a moment of peace in weeks that can sometimes feel chaotic. Physically kneading the dough can help release outside frustrations and give space for mental freewheeling; likewise, the rhythmic process can absorb your attention and help you to be present in the task. For this meditative activity to result in something our trainees are proud to feed their families, we believe there is something remarkably nourishing about bread.

TINA'S STORY

On special occasions, we gather our loved ones together, to honour specific moments in time and share delicious food. For Tina, one of our trainees, the memory of Easter in her Polish homeland brought such a picture of happy times to mind.

In Poland, Easter is family focused, full of traditions and collective preparations for the day ahead. For Tina, the centrepiece of it all was *chałka* bread – a Jewish plaited enriched loaf, full of rich, buttery flavours. According to tradition, once the *chałka* dough had been blessed by the church, everyone had to dance for the time it was baking in the oven. If you sat down at any point, the fear was that the *chałka* would also sit and go flat! With dance and laughter filling the kitchen, the dough would 'come alive'!

What makes this bread so special is the fact that it is enjoyed only once a year. It was a time that Tina looked forward to and a memory that still fills her with joy.

'I was six years old when I first experienced chałka. I was at home with my mum, dad, sister and brother. It was magical: the smell, the dancing and laughter.'

But life isn't always so magical. Years later, Tina found herself homeless when her landlord ended her contract so that he could upgrade the living space. With no place to go and no financially viable options, Tina began to live on the streets of London. After five months with no safe shelter, yet not a priority for council housing, she found a homeless hostel for temporary refuge. Life was bleak and she began to believe that there was no way out. It wasn't until she saw an advertisement for a baking course with Luminary that things started to turn around.

Tina didn't start our programme with the kind of confidence needed to experiment with baking methods and flavours. Prior to starting, she described herself as anxious and hesitant. But as the course progressed and her knowledge of baking grew, so did her excitement and creativity to explore. This new-found confidence brought us the recipes she contributed to this book.

One of the modules taught on the course is breadmaking. Tina thought it was going to be difficult, but found it came naturally to her. It had such an impact that, after graduation, she went on to train at a London bread bakery, refining her skills and mastering her knowledge and understanding of this everyday staple.

To this day, Tina returns to Luminary to teach bread lessons to our trainees. This honour of returning as a teacher to where she was once a trainee is an experience she finds powerful and a process we find to be fully restorative.

'Luminary is a provider in so many ways. They have fed my body, spirit, dreams and imagination as to what's possible in the future. I'm certainly a different person – I'm brand new!'

TINA'S

Chalka Bread

Dust off your Polish mazurka costume and gather your friends and family. This loaf of bread is the perfect focal point for discovering sweet, lively memories. Tina has put her own spin on this Easter recipe – you can enjoy it at any time of the year!

MAKES 1 MEDIUM LOAF

For the loaf
60ml whole milk
50g caster sugar
55g unsalted butter, softened
¼ tsp fine salt
1 x 7g sachet of fast-action
   dried yeast

1 tbsp warm water
¼ tsp vanilla extract
1 medium egg, beaten
175g strong white flour,
   plus extra for dusting
40g raisins or sultanas
1 tbsp vegetable or
   sunflower oil,
   for greasing

**For the crumble topping
(optional)**
25g cold butter, cubed
40g plain flour
4 tsp caster sugar

Warm the milk in a large saucepan over a low heat until lukewarm (about the same temperature as your finger), but don't let it boil. Remove the pan from the heat, then stir in the sugar, softened butter and salt.

In a small bowl, mix the dried yeast with the warm water, then pour the mixture into the milk mixture, along with the vanilla and half of the beaten egg and whisk together. There might still be some small lumps of butter – this is okay.

Add 100g of the flour to the mixture and beat with a wooden spoon until completely smooth with no floury lumps. Stir in the remaining flour and dried fruit.

Tip the sticky dough out onto a lightly floured work surface and knead for 5–10 minutes until smooth and elastic. Alternatively, you can use an electric mixer fitted with a dough hook to do all the messy kneading for you. You'll be able to tell when it's ready by holding a little piece of dough up to a light or window and stretching it between your fingers. If you can stretch the dough thin enough that you can see the light through it without it tearing, it's done! This is called the 'windowpane test'.

Grease a large bowl with the oil and tip the dough into it, turning to coat it in the oil. Cover the bowl with a damp tea towel or clingfilm and leave in a warm place for 60–90 minutes until the dough is doubled in size.

Punch the dough back down inside the bowl, then divide into 3 equal pieces. Roll each piece of dough into a long sausage, about 30cm long and 2cm wide. Join the strands of dough together at one end with a dab of the remaining beaten egg and plait them. At this point, you can either leave it as one long plait or spiral it into a round loaf shape. Transfer it to a baking tray lined with baking paper, cover and leave in a warm place for 60–90 minutes until doubled in size again.

Meanwhile, preheat the oven to 200°C/180°C fan/Gas Mark 6.

If making the crumble topping, rub the butter into the flour until it looks like breadcrumbs, then stir through the sugar. With a pastry brush (or your fingers), brush the top of the loaf with the remaining beaten egg and, if using, sprinkle the crumble across the top.

Bake in the oven for 25–30 minutes until golden brown. (Dancing in the kitchen while it's baking isn't mandatory, but it's a good laugh!)

Leave to cool and enjoy sliced with butter, jam or on its own.

TIP

Lots of bakers use a simple piece of equipment called a 'bench scraper' to help make bread. It's a rectangle of plastic or metal, usually with one curved and one straight edge, used to divide doughs, scrape them off surfaces and help knead. If you're making lots of bread, particularly very wet doughs such as focaccia, you might find investing in one makes a world of difference.

Buttered New Potato and Garden Herb Focaccia

When it comes to baking different breads, the stickier your dough is, the softer the finished product will be. For those willing to embrace the mess, the reward of our beautifully soft and pillowy focaccia is well worth getting your hands completely covered in dough for!

MAKES 1 LARGE LOAF (6–8 LARGE SQUARES)

For the dough
560g strong white flour
2 tsp (11g) fine salt
2½ x 7g sachets (17g) of
    fast-action dried yeast
450ml hand-hot water
2 tbsp olive oil, plus extra
    for greasing

For the topping
300g new potatoes
50g unsalted butter, melted
    (substitute dairy-free
    spread if you want to
    make this vegan)
50ml olive oil
a few fresh rosemary stalks
    (about 10g), picked into
    small sprigs
a few fresh thyme sprigs
    (about 5g), with any
    woody stems removed
a small handful of sage
    (about 10g),
    leaves picked and
    roughly chopped
3 tbsp fresh or dried oregano
    (about 5g)
1 tbsp flaky sea salt

Weigh the strong flour into a large mixing bowl. Add the salt to one side of the bowl and the yeast to the other, making sure they don't touch (if the yeast comes into direct contact with the salt it can retard it and stop your focaccia from rising). Toss the salt in some of the flour surrounding it and do the same with the yeast, finally mixing it all together until combined.

Make a well in the middle of the flour and pour in the warm water and olive oil. Using a bench scraper or wooden spoon, mix the liquids into the flour until a sloppy dough forms and there are no lumps of flour left.

Oil your hands with a little olive oil and tip the wet dough out onto a clean work surface. Knead for 10–15 minutes, stopping to scrape down the worktop every few minutes and bringing it back together. Don't be afraid of how sticky it is – avoid the temptation to add extra flour to the table, your hands or the dough. Alternatively, you can use an electric mixer fitted with a dough hook to do all the messy kneading for you.

After kneading, the dough should be more supple and holding itself together. Transfer it to an oiled bowl, cover with a damp tea towel or clingfilm and place somewhere warm for about 1 hour until it has doubled in size.

Once the dough has doubled in size, line a 30 x 25cm baking tin with baking paper and rub a tablespoon of oil over the tin and your hands. Push the risen dough down, knocking it back inside the bowl, before scraping and tipping it into the lined tin.

Roll the dough around inside the oiled tin so it's glistening with oil, then take the edges of the dough and gently pull, push and wobble it into the corners of the baking tin without tearing it. Fold all the edges of the dough into the middle and turn it upside down to hide all the ugly bits and give you a nice supple, stretched top. Cover the tin with a tea towel/clingfilm and leave to rise in a warm place once again for 1 hour.

While you're waiting for the dough to prove this second time, thinly slice the new potatoes into 5mm slices and mix with the melted butter, oil and herbs.

When the dough is ready, push your fingers deep into the dough a few times, almost to the bottom of the tray, to create little dimples. Sprinkle the oily potato and herb topping over the top of the dough, followed by the sea salt flakes. Leave to prove in a warm place for a final 15 minutes.

Meanwhile, preheat the oven to 220°C/200°C fan/Gas Mark 7.

When the oven is hot, bake the focaccia for 20–25 minutes until golden brown and puffy.

Leave to cool a little before cutting into squares. This bread makes a mean sandwich or is a great accompaniment to meats and cheeses. Our café makes toasties from it every day, slicing the large squares in half and stuffing them with tasty fillings.

MIMI'S
Goat's Cheese and Grape Focaccia

The joy of focaccia is all the space it gives for toppings! It's a blank canvas, waiting to be topped with whatever delicious ingredients take your fancy. Our bakers make fresh focaccia every day, creatively choosing toppings and regularly coming up with new seasonal flavours.

Mimi, one of our bakers, bounded into Luminary for her shift one day clutching a plastic bag brimming with jewel-like black grapes from the vines in her garden, and they inspired the day's focaccia. We love how the grapes glisten and burst with sweet-sour juice as you bite into them, deliciously complementing the creamy goat's cheese and heady olive oil.

MAKES 1 LARGE LOAF (6–8 LARGE PIECES)

For the dough
560g strong white flour
2 tsp (11g) fine salt
2½ x 7g sachets (17g) of fast-action dried yeast
450ml hand-hot water

2 tbsp olive oil, plus extra for greasing

For the topping
250g black, seedless grapes
a good handful of fresh rosemary (about 15g), sprigs picked
50ml olive oil

100g soft goat's cheese, sliced into small chunks
1 tbsp flaky sea salt

Follow the same method for making the dough as for the focaccia on page 32, up until the dough is proving for a second time in its oiled baking tin.

Meanwhile, mix the grapes and rosemary in a bowl with the olive oil and set aside. Slice the goat's cheese into 2cm pieces.

When the dough is ready, push your fingers deep into the dough a few times, almost to the bottom of the tin, to create little dimples. Sprinkle the grapes, rosemary and oil across the top of the dough, followed by the goat's cheese and sea salt flakes. Leave to prove in a warm place for a final 15 minutes.

Meanwhile, preheat the oven to 220°C/200°C fan/Gas Mark 7.

Bake the focaccia for 20–25 minutes until golden brown and puffy.

Leave to cool a little before cutting into squares. This is really good served alongside a cheese platter or cut into small squares as appetisers.

Chive-Marbled Rye Bread

When it comes to bread, Tina is Luminary's queen of it. Her fun-loving nature and ambitious dreaming are what brought together these delicious flavours. Rye bread was a part of her Polish upbringing, but she wanted to mix things up by adding a personal touch: 'We always had chives in my family as there was an excess of them in the garden! Not liking to see things go to waste, I decided to layer them into the bread mix and it turned out pretty swell!' This soft loaf with its beautiful, green swirls will bring a savoury twist to any home-cooked meal, and is especially good with chicken soup or borscht.

MAKES 1 LOAF

310g strong white flour,
     plus extra for dusting
155g white rye flour
2½ tsp (12g) fine salt

3¼ tsp (10g) fast-action
     dried yeast
300ml hand-hot water
2 tbsp vegetable or
     sunflower oil, plus
     a little extra for greasing

2 tsp black treacle
40g fresh chives,
     very finely chopped

Weigh the flours into a large bowl and add the salt to one side of the bowl and the yeast to the other, making sure they don't touch (see page 32). Toss the salt in the flour surrounding it, do the same with the yeast, and finally mix together until combined.

Make a well in the middle of the flour and pour in the warm water, oil and treacle. Mix until the mixture comes together but is still a messy clump and not yet a fully formed dough. Cover with a damp tea towel and leave to rest for 20 minutes.

Tip the half-formed dough onto a lightly floured work surface and knead for about 10 minutes until it becomes elastic and stops sticking to the surface, regularly scraping down the surface with a bench scraper. Alternatively, use an electric mixer fitted with a dough hook to do all the messy kneading for you.

Divide the dough in half and knead the chives into one half until evenly distributed. Place the two doughs in separate oiled bowls, cover with a damp tea towel or clingfilm and leave in a warm place for about 1 hour, or until doubled in size.

Meanwhile, line the base of a 900g/2lb loaf tin with baking paper and brush the sides with a little oil.

Turn the plain dough out onto a lightly floured work surface and roll out into a rectangle, about 25 x 20cm. Brush the surface of the dough with water. Roll the chive dough out to the same size and lay it on top of the plain dough, using the water as 'glue' between them.

Take one of the short sides of dough and fold it over by 1cm, then gently continue to roll the dough into a tight swirl, using your fingers and thumbs to work from one side to the other, rolling as tightly as possible. You should be left with a sausage of dough, about 20cm long. Shape the dough into a loaf to fit the tin and tuck the ends under, then place it in the tin and cover with a damp tea towel or clingfilm. Set aside to prove in a warm place for 30–40 minutes until doubled in size again.

Meanwhile, preheat the oven to 230°C/210°C fan/Gas Mark 8.

Slash the top of the risen loaf with a small sharp knife (Tina makes 5 diagonal cuts). Place it in the oven and immediately reduce the heat to 220°C/200°C fan/ Gas Mark 7. Bake for 40–45 minutes until it is golden brown and sounds hollow when taken out of the tin and tapped on the bottom.

Leave to cool completely before slicing. It's best eaten on the same day.

Olive, Paprika and Manchego Breadsticks

Our doughy batons are made for dipping and ripping, to be part of a tapas feast or served alongside fresh salads. Inspired by the flavours and colours of Spain, we're particularly fond of the way the paprika colours the dough to a warming red-orange hue and brings a smoky sweetness to the bread.

MAKES 18–20

200g plain flour, plus extra
    for dusting
200g strong white flour
3 tsp smoked paprika

2 tsp (10g) fine salt
1¼ tsp (4g) fast-action
    dried yeast
250ml warm water
1 tbsp olive oil, plus extra
    for greasing and brushing

100g black Kalamata
    olives, sliced (or any
    black olives are good)
50g Manchego cheese,
    grated, plus extra
    for sprinkling

In a large bowl, mix together the two flours with the smoked paprika. Add the salt to one side of the bowl and the yeast to the other, making sure they don't touch. Toss the salt in some of the flour surrounding it and do the same with the yeast, finally mixing them all together until well combined. Make a well in the middle of the flour and pour in the warm water and olive oil. Mix together to form a sticky, messy dough.

Tip the dough out onto a clean work surface and knead for about 10 minutes until smooth and supple.

Flatten out the dough, cover the surface with the sliced olives and grated cheese, then fold them into the dough. Knead until the olives and cheese are well dispersed throughout the dough.

Lightly grease the mixing bowl with a little oil, then put the ball of dough back into it and cover with a damp tea towel or clingfilm.

Leave the dough to prove somewhere warm for about 1 hour, or until it has doubled in size.

Oil a couple of baking trays.

Liberally dust the work surface with flour and tip the dough out onto it. Roll the dough out into a large rectangle, about 1cm thick, adding more flour when necessary.

Use a large knife to cut the dough into strips, 1–2cm thick, and transfer them to the oiled baking trays. Make sure to arrange them at least 5cm apart to avoid them touching when they bake.

Brush the top of each strip with a little olive oil, using a pastry brush or your fingers, and sprinkle with more grated Manchego.

Leave the breadsticks to prove in a warm place for a further 30 minutes.

Meanwhile, preheat the oven to 200°C/180°C fan/ Gas Mark 6.

Bake the breadsticks for 20–25 minutes until golden brown. Leave to cool on a wire rack before serving as you like, with dips or salads.

OUR SIGNATURE
English Muffins with Liz's Kumquat and Rosemary Marmalade

Our Liz is many things: an advocate, a leader, a whizz at business operations, a hospitality curator and now a Luminary trustee. She arrived on the scene when Luminary was only a few months old and has been one of our biggest 'cheerleaders' since. The combination of our English muffins with her Kumquat and Rosemary Marmalade (page 42) perfectly sums up how she makes our world that much sweeter.

MAKES 12 MUFFINS

210ml water
210ml buttermilk

1 x 7g sachet of fast-action
    dried yeast
1 tbsp (12g) caster sugar
25ml vegetable oil, plus
    extra for greasing

115g unsalted butter,
    softened
500g strong white flour
2 tsp (10g) fine salt
fine cornmeal, for dusting

Heat the water and buttermilk in a small saucepan until lukewarm (the same temperature as your finger and no hotter). Stir in the yeast and sugar and set aside for 10 minutes. After that time, stir in the oil and butter in chunks.

In a large bowl, mix the flour and salt. Make a well in the middle, add the liquids and bring together into a sticky dough.

Knead the dough on a clean work surface for 10 minutes, using a bench scraper to keep the surface clean and avoiding dusting it with additional flour (extra flour will give you hard and tough muffins). It'll be very sticky so try slapping it on the work surface and folding it over repeatedly, to keep it from covering every inch of the surface. Alternatively, you can use an electric mixer fitted with a dough hook to do all the messy kneading for you.

Place the dough back into the bowl and cover with clingfilm or a damp tea towel. Leave it to prove somewhere warm for 30 minutes. After this time, transfer the bowl to the fridge and prove for a further 1 hour until the dough has doubled in size.

Line 2 large baking trays with baking paper and dust with a thin layer of cornmeal.

Oil your work surface, tip the dough out onto it and cut the dough into 12 equal pieces (about 90g each). Flatten each piece into a 5cm circle and fold the outside edges into the centre, pinching them together. Turn the balls upside down (so the ugly pinched bit is on the bottom and the top is nice and smooth) and place on the baking trays. Dust the muffin tops with a little extra cornmeal and loosely cover both trays with oiled clingfilm. Leave to prove at room temperature for another 45–60 minutes until doubled in size.

Preheat the oven to 160°C/140°C fan/Gas Mark 3, preheat a large frying pan over a low heat and place a third, unlined baking tray in the oven to heat up.

Carefully transfer 3–4 muffins upside down into the hot pan, using a couple of fish slices or spatulas to lift them so that they maintain their shape. Cook for 10 minutes until they have golden brown bottoms, then flip each muffin and cook for a further 5–6 minutes. Patience is everything here – let the muffins slowly brown and cook through or you'll have raw middles.

Transfer the cooked muffins to the baking tray in the hot oven and bake for a further 10 minutes. Once cooked, they'll spring back to the touch and feel light.

Leave to cool for 15 minutes before slicing open and serving with salted butter and your new favourite condiment... (see the recipe overleaf).

(see the recipe overleaf).

TIP
If you can't find buttermilk, you can substitute it for a mixture of 140g natural yoghurt and 70g whole milk.

LIZ'S
Kumquat and Rosemary Marmalade

Essential for spreading on our muffins (page 40), this is also brilliant on toast or spread between the layers of a sponge cake.

MAKES 6 X 170G JARS

1kg kumquats
225ml water, plus 1.5 litres
1kg caster sugar
1 tsp finely chopped
    fresh rosemary

Slice the kumquats into 5mm rounds, removing and reserving any pips. Place the pips in a small bowl with 225ml water and place the kumquat slices in a larger bowl with 1.5 litres water. Cover both and leave to soak overnight in the fridge.

Preheat the oven to 120°C/100°C fan/Gas Mark 1. Sterilise your glass jars and lids (see page 47).

Strain the soaking liquid from the pips into a large saucepan and add the kumquats and their soaking liquid. Bring to the boil, then reduce to a simmer. Cover and simmer for 10–15 minutes until the kumquats are very tender. Remove the lid and keep simmering until the volume is reduced by half.

Meanwhile, warm the sugar in the oven on a small baking tray for 15 minutes. Tip the warm sugar and chopped rosemary into the saucepan and stir until the sugar is fully dissolved. Bring the mixture back to a rapid boil for 15 minutes.

Remove from the heat and transfer the marmalade to a jug. Carefully pour it into the warm, sterilised jars, filling them to about 5mm from the top. Tightly seal the jars and leave to cool completely. They will keep in a cool, dark place for up to 12 months. Once opened, store in the fridge for up to 3 months.

TIPS

Make sure you start the marmalade-making process a day before you'd like to pop a jar open – it needs to soak overnight.

Like other seasonal citrus fruits, kumquats are only readily available in the winter months in England. Once you see them appear in shops, we recommend you stock up and make a few batches of this marmalade to see you through the year.

Crumpets with Rhubarb and Orange Curd

Once you know how, crumpets are so satisfyingly easy to make! Like most homemade treats, they're also a whole lot tastier than the shop-bought version. We love to generously spread our silky Rhubarb and Orange Curd (page 46) over each crumpet, bringing a fruity burst of flavour to every bite. You will need 4–6 metal crumpet or dessert rings, 7cm in diameter, although a round metal cookie cutter will work too.

MAKES 15 CRUMPETS

200ml warm water
20ml whole milk
1 tsp caster sugar
1 x 7g sachet of fast-action
    dried yeast
200g strong white flour
100g plain flour
½ tsp bicarbonate of soda
½ tsp fine salt
25g butter, melted,
    for greasing

Mix the warm water, milk and sugar together in a jug (make sure the mixture is warm but not hot) and stir in the yeast. Set aside for 10–15 minutes until the yeast has become frothy.

In a large mixing bowl, sieve together the flours, bicarbonate of soda and salt and make a well in the middle. Tip in the warm milk and beat into the flour with a wooden spoon to form a smooth batter.

Cover the bowl with a tea towel or clingfilm and leave the batter to prove somewhere warm for 1 hour. It should have small bubbles all over the top when ready.

Thoroughly brush the inside edge of your metal rings and a large frying pan with the melted butter, then heat the frying pan over a medium-low heat until the butter starts to bubble and sizzle. Fit as many metal rings as you can into the pan, sitting them flat on the bottom.

Spoon or pour the batter into the metal rings until each is half filled, then leave to gently cook for 8–10 minutes until the tops are dry to the touch and covered in little holes.

Carefully push the crumpets from their metal rings onto a plate (you may need a knife to loosen them and a tea towel or oven glove to protect your fingers from the heat), then place them back in the pan, upside down, to brown the tops for about 2 minutes.

Reheat and re-grease the pan and rings and repeat the process of filling, cooking and flipping until all the batter has been used up.

Either serve the crumpets warm, or leave to cool on a wire rack and toast before serving, with plenty of butter or our curd (see the recipe on page 46).

Rhubarb and Orange Curd

Curds need to be cooked slowly over a low heat, with constant stirring to prevent the eggs curdling or catching around the edge of the pan. Avoid the temptation to turn up the heat in a moment of impatience. Instead, slowly persist until you have a silky curd that coats the back of a spoon without running off.

MAKES 2 X 250G JARS

400g rhubarb, trimmed and
    chopped into 1cm pieces
finely grated zest of 1 orange
75ml freshly squeezed
    orange juice (from
    about 1 orange)
1 tablespoon water
150g caster sugar
2 tsp cornflour
2 large eggs
50g unsalted butter, cubed
a couple of drops of pink
    food colouring (optional)

Preheat the oven to 120°C/100°C fan/Gas Mark 1. Sterilise 2 glass jam jars by washing the jars and lids in soapy water, rinse well, then place all upside-down on a baking tray and place in the oven for 15 minutes.

Put the chopped rhubarb, orange zest and juice into a small saucepan along with 1 tablespoon water and place over a medium heat. Gently simmer for 10 minutes until the rhubarb is soft and has broken down.

Strain the rhubarb and all the juices through a sieve into a medium saucepan, pressing out any liquid from the rhubarb to leave just the fibres behind in the sieve (discard these).

In a small bowl, whisk together the sugar and cornflour, then crack the eggs into the bowl and whisk them in. Add the mixture to the pan of juices and whisk until smooth. Add the cubed butter and food colouring (if using).

Place the pan over a low heat and gently stir the curd with a wooden spoon for 7–10 minutes, making sure to catch any bits that are cooking from around the edges and bring them into the middle. Keep stirring over a low heat until the mixture is thick enough to coat the back of the spoon – a little thicker than the consistency of custard.

Pour the curd into the sterilised jars and seal with the lids. Leave to cool completely before cracking open to spread on crumpets! It will keep in the fridge for up to 3 weeks.

KENZEY'S STORY

Kenzey struggled to find positive opportunities to pursue a life of independence. Her time in the criminal justice system at a young age meant that by the time of her release she was at a social and economic disadvantage.

But this did not dampen her spirits for a better life. Kenzey always loved baking, so when she saw an article in a magazine about the training offered by Luminary Bakery, she immediately jumped at the chance.

'Because of everything I had been through in my past, I knew that this was a great opportunity to give me more skills to bake, as well as help empower me and give me confidence.'

As Kenzey's confidence grew, so did her excitement in experimenting with different flavours. She no longer felt like her background or inexperience was holding her back as she pulled together basic ingredients like flour, sugar and butter and transformed them into delicious baked goods – baking we saw as outstanding. So much so, that when we held a competition on the course to find a new baked good, Kenzey's Chocolate and Hazelnut Pretzels (see recipe overleaf) had our tastebuds celebrating. We happily chose her as our winner. We loved the inspiration behind her recipe: childhood memories of visiting shopping centres and enjoying a warm pretzel as a treat with her family and friends.

KENZEY'S
Chocolate and Hazelnut Pretzels

As far as breads go, these pretzels are the simple indulgences that dreams are made of – and the perfect on-the-go treat for adults and children alike.

MAKES 8

For the pretzels
450g strong white flour
35g light soft brown sugar
½ tsp fine salt
1 x 7g sachet of fast-action
    dried yeast
275ml warm water

50g unsalted butter, melted
1 tbsp vegetable or sunflower
    oil, for greasing
3 tbsp bicarbonate of soda
1 medium egg, beaten with
    a pinch of salt
50g chopped hazelnuts
flaky sea salt, for sprinkling

For the dipping sauce
60ml whole milk
120g chocolate hazelnut
    spread (we use Nutella)
½ tsp vanilla extract
½ tsp honey

To make the dough, weigh the flour and sugar into a large mixing bowl. Add the salt to one side of the bowl and the yeast to the other, making sure they don't touch (if the yeast comes into direct contact with the salt it can retard it and stop the dough from rising). Toss the salt in some of the flour surrounding it, do the same with the yeast, finally mixing them all together until combined.

Make a well in the middle of the flour and pour in the warm water and melted butter. Mix with a bench scraper or wooden spoon until it comes together into a messy dough. Tip the dough and any remaining flour onto a clean work surface and knead for 10 minutes until smooth and supple. You'll be able to tell when you have kneaded it enough with the 'windowpane test' (see page 31).

Transfer the dough back into the bowl, cover with a damp tea towel or clingfilm and leave to prove in a warm place for about 1 hour until it has doubled in size.

Line a couple of large baking trays with baking paper and grease with a little vegetable or sunflower oil.

Once the dough has risen, knock out any large air bubbles from the dough and divide into 8 equal pieces (weighing about 100g each). Roll each piece of dough into a long sausage, about 30cm long. Make each sausage into a large 'U' shape, cross the ends over one another, then twist them round once before attaching them near to the base of the 'U', making the classic pretzel shape (see illustration).

Once shaped, move the pretzels to the prepared baking trays and leave to prove for 30–40 minutes until doubled in size again.

Meanwhile, preheat the oven to 200°C/180°C fan/ Gas Mark 6.

Pour 1 litre water into a saucepan and bring to the boil. Tip the bicarbonate of soda into the pan and let it bubble up and settle back down. One at a time, gently lower the pretzels into the boiling water and boil for 20 seconds – they should float. Remove the pretzels from the water with a fish slice or flat spatula and carefully lay them back onto the lined baking trays.

Brush the top of each pretzel with the beaten egg and sprinkle with chopped hazelnuts and sea salt flakes. Bake for 20–25 minutes until a deep golden brown.

To make the dipping sauce, warm the milk in a saucepan over a medium heat, then whisk in the chocolate hazelnut spread, vanilla and honey until smooth. Either drizzle the sauce over the baked pretzels or serve it in small dishes alongside the warm pretzels for dunking.

TIP

Brushing breads or pastries with beaten egg before baking gives them a golden brown sheen, but sometimes the egg can be jelly-like and hard to brush on without damaging the dough. To avoid this, beat a pinch of salt into the egg and leave it aside for 5–10 minutes before brushing it on.

Cinnamon Swirls with Cream Cheese Frosting

Our infamously large, gorgeously swirled cinnamon buns are one of our most popular bakes. Nothing compares to a fresh cinnamon bun – fluffy dough spiralled with sweet cinnamon butter and baked until puffy and golden. A few years ago, when we began baking these scrumptious swirls in our very first kitchen, we'd pile them high into large boxes and carry them on the Tube across London to cafés and their hungry customers. You can imagine the looks from commuters as the smell of freshly baked cinnamon pastries filled the carriages! Now, our buns only have to make the short journey from the ovens to our counters at the Luminary Bakeries where they're sold fresh every day, warm and generously piped with luxurious cream cheese frosting.

MAKES 8 LARGE BUNS

For the dough
675g strong white flour, plus
    extra for dusting
70g caster sugar
1½ tsp (7g) fine salt
3¼ tsp (10g) fast-action
    dried yeast
1 medium egg, beaten
400ml whole milk, warmed
    to lukewarm
70g unsalted butter, softened

For the filling
150g unsalted butter,
    softened
75g soft light brown sugar
75g golden syrup
1 tbsp ground cinnamon

For the frosting
50g unsalted butter,
    softened
100g cream cheese,
    at room temperature
200g icing sugar
½ tsp vanilla extract

To make the dough, combine the flour and sugar in a large mixing bowl. Add the salt to one side of the bowl and the yeast to the other, making sure they don't touch. Toss the salt in some of the flour surrounding it and do the same with the yeast, finally mixing them all together until combined. (If the yeast comes into direct contact with the salt it can retard it and stop the buns rising.)

Weigh out 25g of the beaten egg (about half – reserve the other half for an egg wash later) and mix into the warm milk. Make a well in the middle of the flour, pour in the milk mixture and use a butter knife or bench scraper to bring it together into a soft ball of dough. Get your hands involved, kneading it in the bowl before tipping it out onto a clean work surface.

Knead the dough for 10 minutes, using a bench scraper to keep the surface clean. Avoid dusting it with extra flour (this will give you hard, tough buns). It will be very sticky so try slapping it on the work surface and folding it over repeatedly, to keep it from covering every inch of the surface. Alternatively, use an electric mixer fitted with a dough hook to do all the messy kneading for you.

Add the butter to the dough and knead for a further 5 minutes until glossy and still slightly sticky to the touch. Try the 'windowpane test' (see page 31) to be sure it's ready. Return the dough to the mixing bowl, cover with a damp tea towel or clingfilm and leave somewhere warm to prove until doubled in size (1½–2 hours).

Meanwhile, make the filling. In a bowl, mix the butter, sugar, syrup and cinnamon into a smooth paste using a wooden spoon or spatula. Spread about 2 tablespoons of the mixture over the base of a 30 x 25 x 5cm baking tin and set aside.

Once the dough has proved, knock out the excess air by squashing and punching it back into the bowl a few times. Scrape the dough out onto a very well-floured work surface and use a floured rolling pin to roll the dough out into a 60 x 30cm rectangle, about 2cm thick.

Evenly spread the remaining filling mixture across the dough, right to the very edges. Find the shortest edge of dough and fold over 1cm of it, then continue to gently roll the dough up into a tight swirl, using your fingers and thumbs to work from one side to the other. Roll it as tightly as possible. You should be left with a dough sausage about 30cm in length.

Mark out, then use a very sharp knife to cut the sausage of dough into 8 even slices. Place the slices, swirl-side facing up, on the cinnamon-smeared baking tin, spacing them about 2–3cm apart. Leave somewhere warm for 40–60 minutes to prove a second time, covered with a damp tea towel or clingfilm. They should have doubled in size and started to touch one another.

Meanwhile, preheat the oven to 200°C/180°C fan/Gas Mark 6.

Brush the top of each swirl with the remaining beaten egg, then bake for 20–25 minutes until golden brown. Once baked, transfer the tin to a wire rack and let them cool completely in the tin.

To make the frosting, beat together the softened butter and cream cheese with an electric mixer or spatula until smooth. Add the icing sugar in 3 stages, mixing in each third before adding the next. Once it's smooth and creamy, mix in the vanilla extract. Spoon the frosting into a piping bag and pipe zigzags over the top of each cooled bun. If you don't have a piping bag, don't worry – you can use a spoon to drizzle or smear the frosting over the tops of the buns instead. Enjoy!

'Hospitality is "love on the loose".
It means more than an occasion to
cook and consume, but to create
a welcoming space to empower
friendship, purpose and unity.
With that, you are encompassing
the very best of the things that
Luminary represents.'

LIZ, LUMINARY TRUSTEE
AND DIRECTOR

QUICK
BREADS

As the name suggests, quick breads are surprisingly *quick* to make. Unlike yeasted breads, they don't require kneading or proving, so their doughs or batters can be made and put straight in the oven to bake. They rely on baking powder or bicarbonate of soda instead of yeast to make them rise, so in place of yeast's familiar taste we pack in plenty of punchy flavours – think gooey cheese, roasted garlic, zesty orange and warming cider.

These quick breads are a blessing on days where you don't have the time to wait around for homemade bread to be ready. And with mixing and shaping being the only skills required to make a loaf (and sometimes not even that!), they're much easier to master, too. You'll be whipping up a loaf in next to no time!

Better still, lots of quick breads don't need gluten (the stretchy protein found in flour) to give them their structure, so they can be easily adapted to use gluten-free (GF) flour. GF breads can be harder to come by, so coeliacs or those on GF diets will find a few recipes in this chapter to enjoy.

TRACEY'S STORY

Some people you meet in life just *sparkle*. From the first day we met Tracey, she captivated us with her stories. She grew with us just as we grew as an organisation with her – in animation, experience and boldness. A graduate of our first cohort, she has influenced Luminary's journey. Hers is, simply put, a story of rising hope!

Tracey spent a large part of her life in a home darkened by domestic violence. She was kept secluded away from the bright world outside and driven into a life of forced isolation. There were rare moments of genuine human connection and what she thought, liked or disliked was not heard or even acknowledged. When she finally escaped, homelessness was the only option and she sought refuge in a hostel. While there, she was invited to a baking course at Luminary.

'Luminary, for me, was a godsend. They gave me confidence and courage and a voice to speak. I hadn't spoken for two years, but then I came to Luminary. They gave me hope where there was no hope.'

Tracey eventually found her voice during the course at Luminary. Being around women who had similar backgrounds and living conditions drew out confidence and gave her a community of women to learn from and be encouraged by. During our personal and professional group sessions where the women learn how to grow in confidence and perception of their self-worth, Tracey began to find her voice. It wasn't easy at the time, and some days it felt daunting, but the support and space Tracey received helped her to process the past and seek a new hope for the future. Tracey began to trust again.

Although Tracey classified her first attempts at baking as 'disastrous', she remained determined. As an avid cook, she quickly realised that baking relied on using specific measurements. Accuracy was key. Hers wasn't just a dedication to learn, but a courageous fight for a new and better life.

'Luminary is love, trust, hope and life!
You come in broken and you go out like a firework!'

Carrot Bread with Nigella Seeds

Inspired by Tracey's radiant story of perseverance (page 60), our carrot bread really does glow! Packed with orange carrots and yellow turmeric, it's a sunny recipe that will brighten the day of anyone who eats a slice... or two!

MAKES 1 LOAF

50g unsalted butter, plus extra
    for greasing
1 small onion, finely chopped
½ tsp ground coriander
½ tsp ground cumin
¼ tsp ground turmeric
1 tsp nigella seeds, plus extra
    for sprinkling
150g gluten-free white flour
    (we use Doves Farm)
100g fine polenta or cornmeal
1½ tsp gluten-free baking powder
½ tsp fine salt
½ tsp cracked black pepper
3 medium eggs
150ml whole milk
2 carrots (about 200g), grated

Preheat the oven to 180°C/160°C fan/Gas Mark 4. Grease and line a 900g/2lb loaf tin (23 x 13 x 7cm) with 2 strips of baking paper, arranged in a cross shape overlapping on the base of the tin, to line every side.

Melt the butter in a small saucepan over a medium heat, then add the chopped onion and gently fry for 5–10 minutes. Add the ground coriander, cumin, turmeric and nigella seeds and cook, stirring, for 1 minute. Once they're soft and golden brown, set the onions aside to cool.

Sift the flour, polenta, baking powder, salt and pepper into a large bowl and stir to mix.

In a separate medium bowl, whisk together the eggs and milk, then stir in the cooled onion and grated carrots.

Make a well in the middle of the dry ingredients and pour in the carrot mixture. Using a large spoon or spatula, bring the flour into the middle of the bowl, mixing it all together to form a batter. Once all the flour is incorporated, stop mixing and pour the batter into the lined loaf tin. Sprinkle a small handful of nigella seeds over the top.

Bake in the oven for 40–45 minutes until golden brown and an inserted skewer or knife comes out clean.

Leave the bread to cool in the tin for 5 minutes before tipping out onto a wire rack to cool completely. This is delicious eaten warm, spread with butter or dunked in soup.

TIP

This bread is designed to work with gluten-free flour for those on gluten-free diets, but works just as well with plain wheat flour.

Cauliflower Cheese Savoury Muffins

Our moreish muffins contain all the comfort of cauliflower cheese on a lazy Sunday afternoon, livened up with warming spices and mustard. We should warn you though, once you've had one it's hard to resist going back for a second...

MAKES 12

80g unsalted butter
1 small–medium onion, finely chopped
1 tsp mustard powder
1 tsp mild curry powder
1 tsp black mustard seeds

275g natural yoghurt
100ml whole milk
2 medium eggs
250g plain flour (gluten-free flour works here too)
2 tsp baking powder
½ tsp bicarbonate of soda
1½ tsp fine salt

100g mature Cheddar cheese, grated, plus a little extra to sprinkle on top
250g cauliflower, roughly cut into 1–2cm pieces
cracked black pepper

Preheat the oven to 200°C/180°C fan/Gas Mark 6 and line a 12-hole muffin tin with paper cases.

Melt the butter in a small frying pan over a medium heat, add the onion and gently fry for 5–10 minutes until soft and golden brown. Sprinkle the mustard powder, curry powder and black mustard seeds over the onion and fry for a further 2 minutes, stirring regularly. Set aside to cool.

In a medium bowl, whisk together the yoghurt, milk and eggs, then stir in the cooled onion.

In a large bowl, sift together the flour, baking powder, bicarbonate of soda and salt, then stir in the grated cheese and chopped cauliflower. Make a well in the middle of the mixture and pour in the wet ingredients. Using a large spoon or spatula, bring the flour into the middle of the bowl, mixing it all together to form a stiff batter. Once all the flour is incorporated, stop mixing – over-mixing will result in rubbery muffins!

Use a dessertspoon or ice-cream scoop to evenly divide the muffin batter among the paper cases, filling them three-quarters full. Sprinkle over a little extra cheese and crack some black pepper over the top of each one.

Bake for 18–20 minutes until the muffins are golden brown and they spring back when gently pressed.

Roasted Garlic Irish Soda Bread

We have to thank our former Head Baker Aine, with her resourcefulness and Irish roots, for introducing us to the wonders of Irish soda bread. We sell loaves of it at our café in Stoke Newington every day (usually still warm from the oven) and our customers often tell us that they can smell it cooking from down the street! It is one of the most versatile breads out there – you can add almost any ingredients you like. It is best eaten on the day that it's made, but makes great toast for days afterwards, especially when slathered in salted butter.

MAKES 1 LOAF

1 bulb of garlic
1 tbsp olive oil
420ml buttermilk
    (or 300g natural yoghurt
    and 120ml whole milk
    mixed together)

250g wholemeal plain flour
250g plain flour, plus extra
    for dusting
1 tsp bicarbonate of soda
1 tsp fine salt
1 tsp cracked black pepper

Preheat the oven to 200°C/180°C fan/Gas Mark 6 and line a baking tray with baking paper.

Cut the top off the garlic bulb to just about reveal the cloves inside, leaving the papery skin on. Place the bulb in a small baking tin, drizzle with the olive oil and bake in the oven for 20–30 minutes until the cloves are soft to the touch. Set aside to cool.

When cool, squeeze the roasted garlic out of each papery casing and into a separate bowl. Mash it up into a paste with a fork or press it through a garlic press, then mix in the buttermilk and whisk together.

In a large bowl, mix together the flours, bicarbonate of soda, salt and pepper, making sure the salt and bicarbonate of soda are well distributed throughout the flour.

Make a well in the middle of the flour mixture and pour in the buttermilk mixture. Use your hands, a spatula or bench scraper to mix the wet ingredients into the dry until a sticky dough forms.

Lightly flour a work surface and tip the dough onto it. Gently roll and fold the dough a couple of times to bring the mixture together. Do not knead – you just want to bring it together.

Shape the dough into a ball and transfer it to the baking tray. Gently press down with your hands to flatten the ball into a disc, about 5cm thick. Liberally dust the top with flour and use a large sharp knife to score the dough with a deep cross dividing it into quarters, about 2cm deep. A 'sawing' action can help get a sharp cut.

Bake for 35–40 minutes until golden brown and hollow-sounding when turned upside-down and knocked on the bottom. Once baked, leave to cool on a wire rack.

TIP
This roasted garlic version is a favourite of ours, but if garlic isn't your thing, try adding 200g of crumbled Stilton and 100g of roasted walnuts instead – it's just as delicious and the oozy cheese is such a treat!

Oat Milk Soda Bread

We love everything about soda bread: it's quick, easy and cheap to make; it's a great use for milk that's turned sour; and there's no kneading or proving required due to the absence of yeast. Usually, because of the lack of yeast that brings flavour to bread, it relies on tangy buttermilk as an ingredient – but we've developed this recipe using oat milk instead, so those on dairy-free diets can enjoy it too!

MAKES 1 LOAF

350ml oat milk
40ml lemon juice

220g plain flour, plus extra for dusting
220g wholemeal flour
75g rolled oats, plus an extra handful to sprinkle on top

1½ tsp bicarbonate of soda
1 tsp salt

Preheat the oven to 200°C/180°C fan/Gas Mark 6 and line a large baking tray with baking paper.

In a small bowl, combine the oat milk with the lemon juice and stir. Set aside for about 10 minutes to allow it to curdle slightly.

Weigh the flours into a large bowl, then add the oats, bicarbonate of soda and salt. Using your hands, rub the dry ingredients together, making sure the salt and bicarbonate of soda are evenly distributed throughout the flour.

Make a well in the middle of the dry ingredients and pour in the curdled oat milk. Begin to fold the dry and wet ingredients together using a spatula or bench scraper. The dough will feel very messy and possibly quite sticky, but avoid the temptation to add more flour. Keep on mixing until it resembles a rough, messy dough.

Flour your hands, turn the dough out onto a clean, well-floured work surface and bring the dough together into a ball. Transfer the ball of dough to the lined baking tray and flatten it with the palm of your hand to about 5cm thick. Sprinkling the top with more flour if it's sticking to your hands. Sprinkle a handful of oats over the top of the loaf.

Use a sharp knife to cut a deep cross into the loaf, about two-thirds of the way through, but not all the way to the tray. A 'sawing' action can help get a sharp cut. Leave to rest for 5 minutes.

Bake in the oven for 30 minutes until golden brown, well risen and the loaf sounds hollow when turned upside-down and tapped. Cool on a wire rack.

Pumpkin and Chilli Cornbread Muffins

Abby is one of the founding Luminary bakers and worked tirelessly to establish and run our first kitchen. She's particularly talented at making mouthwatering recipes for those with food intolerances and allergies. These golden muffins, influenced by her American upbringing, are testament to that – free from gluten, eggs, dairy, soy, nuts and refined sugar – and yet absolutely packed full of flavour. There's no better companion to a big pot of chilli.

MAKES 12

60ml vegetable oil, plus extra for greasing
250ml plant-based milk (you could use cashew, almond, soy, oat... we use coconut)
2 tsp apple cider vinegar

2 red chillies (we use bird's-eye chillies)
175g fine cornmeal, plus extra for sprinkling
150g gluten-free plain flour
½ tsp bicarbonate of soda
1½ tsp gluten-free baking powder
¾ tsp fine salt

35g coconut sugar or caster sugar
85g pumpkin purée (see tip)
55g maple syrup, plus extra to serve (optional)

Preheat the oven to 175°C/155°C fan/Gas Mark 3 and brush the holes of a 12-hole muffin tin with a little oil.

In a small bowl, mix together the plant milk and apple cider vinegar and set aside for 5–10 minutes.

Meanwhile, carefully cut one of the chillies into thin rings, discard the seeds and set the rings aside to decorate the top of the muffins. De-seed and finely chop the second chilli.

In a large bowl, mix together the cornmeal, flour, bicarbonate of soda, baking powder, salt and sugar.

In a separate bowl, mix together the pumpkin purée, vegetable oil and maple syrup with the milk and vinegar mixture.

Make a well in the middle of the dry ingredients and pour in the wet ingredients, mixing them until only a few lumps remain. Gently stir through the finely chopped chilli and spoon the batter into the greased muffin tin, filling each hole about three-quarters full. Sprinkle the top of each with a little extra cornmeal and place a chilli ring on top.

Bake in the oven for 18–20 minutes until the muffins spring back to the touch and an inserted toothpick comes out clean.

Leave to cool in the tin for 5 minutes before tipping them out onto a wire rack to cool completely. Alternatively, eat warm drizzled with a little maple syrup.

TIP

You can use canned pumpkin or make your own pumpkin purée. To make your own: peel and cut a small pumpkin into 2.5cm chunks. Steam it for 15–20 minutes until a fork slides through it easily without resistance. Add the pumpkin to a blender and gradually take the speed from low to high until it is puréed. Alternatively, use a potato masher to mash the pumpkin into a smooth purée.

OUR SIGNATURE
Cheese Scones
with Marmite Butter

Our Head Baker Rachel had one thing on her mind when planning the bakes for our first café: cheese scones. Really big, really fluffy, seriously cheesy scones. And they quickly became a firm favourite at Luminary. By nature, they're wonderfully quick and simple to make – an easy crowd pleaser that are both endearing and impressive to be pulling out of the oven if you have guests. Serve them warm and slathered with Marmite butter for a salty, savoury treat.

MAKES 12

For the scones
900g plain flour, plus extra
    for dusting
2 tbsp baking powder
1 tsp fine salt
1 tsp mustard powder
a generous pinch of
    cayenne pepper

100g unsalted butter, chilled,
    cut into 1cm cubes
250g mature Cheddar
    cheese, grated
280ml whole milk
280ml cold water
1 medium egg, beaten,
    or 1 tbsp milk, for glazing
cracked black pepper

For the Marmite butter
150g salted butter, softened
    at room temperature
40g Marmite (or other
    yeast extract)

Preheat the oven to 180°C/160°C fan/Gas Mark 4 and line a large baking tray with baking paper.

In a large bowl, mix together the flour, baking powder, salt, mustard powder and cayenne pepper. Add the cubed butter and use your fingertips to rub the butter into the flour until only a few small lumps remain and it looks a bit like breadcrumbs. Stir in 200g of the grated cheese.

Make a well in the middle of the dry mixture and pour in the milk and cold water. Use a blunt butter knife to stir the dry mixture into the liquids until it starts to form a soft dough.

Once it's nearly combined, get your hands involved. Bring the dough together into a ball and tip out onto a floured work surface, getting every last bit of flour out of the bowl. It might be stickier than you'd expect, but avoid the temptation to add more flour.

Liberally dust a rolling pin with flour and roll out the dough to about 4cm thick. Use a 9cm round cutter to cut out circles of dough and place them on the lined baking tray, about 5cm apart. Re-roll the scraps until you have used up all the dough.

Brush the top of each scone with beaten egg or milk and sprinkle with the remaining 50g of grated cheese and some freshly cracked black pepper.

Bake for 20–25 minutes until well-risen and golden brown.

While the scones are in the oven, prepare the Marmite butter. Mix together the softened butter and Marmite until marbled and swirly with glossy Marmite streaks.

Once the scones are baked, leave for 5 minutes to cool slightly before serving with the salty savoury butter. They're best eaten on the day they are made, and exceptionally good when warm.

Cider and Apple Bread

There's something striking about this cider and apple bread that'll remind you of the science at work when you bake. Adding the acidic apple cider vinegar to the alkaline bicarbonate of soda sparks a magical instant reaction, producing gas and causing the mixture to foam and swell, leaving you with a light and fluffy loaf. It's a versatile bake that can be eaten at any time of day and becomes sweet or savoury depending on what you choose to serve it with; great for breakfast spread with honey, or lunch alongside warming soups or stews.

MAKES 1 LOAF

vegetable oil, for greasing
500g plain white flour, plus
    extra for dusting
1 tsp bicarbonate of soda
½ tsp ground cinnamon
1 tsp fine salt
1 tsp apple cider vinegar
400ml cider
1 large eating apple
    (or 2 small), grated
    (about 175g)

Preheat the oven to 200°C/180°C fan/Gas Mark 6 and grease and line a 900g/2lb loaf tin (23 x 13 x 7 cm) with 2 strips of baking paper, arranged in a cross shape overlapping on the base to line the sides of the tin.

In a large bowl, mix together the flour, bicarbonate of soda, cinnamon and salt, making sure all the ingredients are evenly distributed throughout.

In a separate bowl, mix together the vinegar, cider and grated apple.

Make a well in the middle of the flour mixture and pour in the apple mixture. Using your hands, a spatula or bench scraper, work quickly to mix the wet ingredients into the dry until a sticky and foaming dough forms.

Tip the foamy batter into the loaf tin without knocking too much of the air out of it and sprinkle the top of the mixture with a handful of flour.

Bake for 35–40 minutes until golden brown and hollow-sounding when turned upside-down and knocked on the bottom. Leave to cool on a wire rack.

This bread is best eaten on the day it's made, but makes great toast for days afterwards.

Cranberry, Orange and White Chocolate Soda Bread

Our former Head Baker Aine had a lasting impact on the Luminary trainees she taught to bake, encouraging self worth and the therapeutic properties of baking. It was in the busy run-up to Christmas that she originally taught this heavenly recipe – it's quick to make and a great loaf for beginners. Packed with tart dried cranberries, orange zest and creamy white chocolate, it's so delicious that we now happily eat it all year round!

MAKES 1 LOAF

250g plain flour, plus extra
    for dusting
250g wholemeal flour
1 tsp bicarbonate of soda
1¼ tsp fine salt
grated zest of 1 orange
100g dried cranberries
100g white chocolate,
    roughly chopped into
    1cm chunks
420ml buttermilk
    (or 300g natural yoghurt
    and 120ml whole milk
    mixed together)

Preheat the oven to 200°C/180°C fan/Gas Mark 6 and line a baking tray with baking paper.

In a large bowl, mix together the flours, bicarbonate of soda, salt, orange zest, dried cranberries and white chocolate chunks, making sure the salt and bicarbonate of soda are well distributed throughout the flour.

Make a well in the middle of the mixture and pour in the buttermilk. Using your hands, a spatula or bench scraper, mix the wet ingredients into the dry until a sticky dough forms.

Lightly flour a work surface and tip the dough out onto it. Gently roll and fold the dough a couple of times to bring the mixture together. Do not knead – you just want to bring it together.

Shape the dough into a ball and transfer to the baking tray, then gently press down on it with your hands to flatten the ball to a disc, about 5cm thick.

Lightly dust the top of the dough with flour and use a large sharp knife to score a deep cross, about 2cm deep, into the top, dividing the dough into quarters.

Bake for 30–35 minutes until golden brown and hollow-sounding when turned upside-down and knocked on the bottom. Leave to cool on a wire rack.

This bread is best eaten on the day it's made, but makes great toast for days afterwards, especially when slathered in some salted butter.

COOKIES
& BISCUITS

As one of the first sweet treats we try as children, cookies and biscuits have a special tie to childhood. Of the many bakes you could choose to make, these are on the simpler side, meaning they can be a fun activity to do with kids or something novice bakers can turn to first. As a result, they joyously form some of our first baking memories –

what a great welcome to this world of flour, butter and sugar!

For this reason, we start the Luminary Baking Programme by making cookies – soft, almost fudgy in the middle and golden and crisp on the outside. They are fun, they are moreish (sometimes *too* moreish), and they'll satisfy that sweet tooth, whatever the time of the day.

KILIAN'S STORY

When Kilian was a child, hot home-cooked meals were rare and there was no one around to explain how to combine ingredients into tasty treats. So, Kilian self-taught the only way a child could, by putting store-bought, ready-made meals in the microwave. This continued into adulthood, but the inner ambition to seek better ways to cook and eat was never far away.

Years later, Kilian joined the Luminary Bakery programme in the hope of a better life. Working alongside our bakery team, the support was a comfort. No longer alone in the learning process, trial-and-error became fun. It was through this collaborative effort that Kilian began to feel a bond with the other trainees. As someone who avoided sharing about the past, Luminary's group sessions offered opportunities for Kilian to process the disadvantage that had been experienced, and also for everyone to walk together in turning their lives around. It created a bond that Kilian called 'breathtaking'.

Now, with a growing desire to discover the most tempting flavour combinations, Kilian doesn't shy away from experimenting, especially when it came to creating the biscuit recipe on page 84. By the time the sixth batch of attempts came through, Kilian said the taste was 'like a choir singing in harmony – several tones coming together for something new'. Kilian took fresh mint buttercream – classier than peppermint – and paired it perfectly with coconut biscuits. We were in awe!

'Luminary is prima *(German for 'great'). I feel respected. I don't feel judged. It's very constructive and positive to do baking. They really believe in me here! Like sand in an oyster, life can feel tough and gritty; there are so many pressures and it's easy to feel as though it's all so hard; so negative; we should just give up. But like an oyster transforms a piece of sand into a beautiful shiny pearl, with a bit of determination, help and support, we can all shine and become something beautiful too... Luminary has been my oyster.'*

Coconut and Fresh Mint Sandwich Biscuits

Simply put, Kilian's biscuits taste like the holidays: soothing, scrumptious and full of memories!

MAKES 15 SANDWICH BISCUITS

For the biscuits
125g unsalted butter, softened
200g icing sugar
1 medium egg
150g plain flour

½ tsp bicarbonate of soda
½ tsp fine salt
100g desiccated coconut, plus extra to decorate

For the buttercream filling
90g unsalted butter, softened
200g icing sugar

1 tbsp whole milk
a tiny dab of green food colouring
2 tbsp finely chopped fresh mint leaves (about 6g)

Beat the softened butter with an electric mixer on a medium speed for a couple of minutes. Tip in the sugar and continue to beat until they are creamed together and the mixture has turned pale and fluffy. Add the egg to the mixture and beat in.

In a small, separate bowl, mix together the flour, bicarbonate of soda, salt and desiccated coconut. Add this dry mixture to the butter mixture in thirds, mixing between each addition, until a soft biscuit dough forms. Cover the bowl with clingfilm and refrigerate for 20–30 minutes.

Meanwhile, preheat the oven to 180°C/160°C fan/Gas Mark 4 and line 2 large baking trays with baking paper.

Weigh the dough into 20g pieces and roll gently into balls between the palms of your hands. You should get 30 balls from the mixture.

Tip some more desiccated coconut into a small bowl and roll each ball of dough around in the coconut until well coated.

Place the balls on the lined baking trays, leaving a gap of at least 5cm between each one to allow them room to spread.

Bake for 10–12 minutes until golden around the edges.

Leave to cool for 10 minutes on the baking tray, before transferring to a wire rack to cool down completely.

To make the buttercream filling, whip the softened butter with an electric mixer on medium speed for a couple of minutes. Add the icing sugar, a spoonful at a time, making sure it's all mixed in before adding the next spoonful. Continue to beat until the mixture becomes pale and fluffy. Add the milk and a tiny amount of green food colouring (less is more!) and mix to get a pale mint-green colour. Finally, mix in the chopped mint leaves.

Fill a piping bag with the buttercream (or just use a small butter knife if you don't have one). Pipe or smear a circle of buttercream on the underside of half of the cooled biscuits, right up to the edge. Fill in the middle of the circle with a little more buttercream and sandwich each one with another biscuit to finish.

Pink Grapefruit and Poppy Seed Biscuits

Buttery and crumbly, these are a tea-time triumph. Grapefruit zest is the zingiest of all the citrus fruits – the flavour dances on your tongue and lingers a little while longer than orange and lemon. This recipe is inspired by biscuits that we used to sell, designed by our very first apprentice, lovingly dug out of the Luminary archives to honour her and all she has achieved since.

MAKES 24

250g unsalted butter, softened
80g caster sugar
50g icing sugar
grated zest of 1 pink grapefruit (although any grapefruit will work well if you can't find a pink one!)

1 medium egg
1½ tsp vanilla extract
330g plain flour, plus extra for dusting
½ tsp fine salt

3 tbsp poppy seeds
2 tbsp granulated sugar

Using an electric mixer, cream together the butter, caster and icing sugars and grapefruit zest until light and fluffy, then beat in the egg and vanilla until fully combined.

On a slow speed, gradually add in the flour, salt and 1 tablespoon of the poppy seeds and gently mix it into a speckled dough. Stop mixing as soon as there's no more flour visible.

Turn the dough out onto a clean, lightly floured work surface and gently roll it into a log shape, about 30 x 10cm. Wrap tightly in clingfilm, twisting it at the ends to pull it tight. Place in the freezer for 30–60 minutes to rest and chill.

Preheat the oven to 180°C/160°C fan/Gas Mark 4 and line 2 baking trays with baking paper.

Tip the granulated sugar and remaining poppy seeds into a baking tray with a rim, unwrap the dough and roll it gently in the mixture to coat the outside.

Use a sharp knife to cut the log into 24 equal slices, each about 1cm thick, and place them on the lined trays at least 5cm apart to allow for spreading.

Bake for 12–15 minutes until golden brown.

Leave the biscuits to cool for 5 minutes on the trays before transferring to a wire rack to cool completely.

SARAH'S
Apricot and Pistachio Thumbprint Biscuits

Steeped in Luminary history, these biscuits were one of many that Sarah made when she, Abby and Alice established our bakery. Having many mouths to feed growing up, Sarah was familiar with baking on a large scale and remained undaunted by the task of rolling hundreds of cookies and biscuits. The first year at Luminary Bakery was chaotic to say the least, yet she consistently led with grace and patience, and remained as cheerful as the sunny pools of apricot sitting atop these biscuits.

MAKES 12

170g unsalted butter,
   softened
110g caster sugar
1 tsp vanilla extract
1 tbsp whole milk
225g plain flour
a pinch of fine salt
50g shelled, unsalted
   pistachios, finely chopped
175g apricot jam

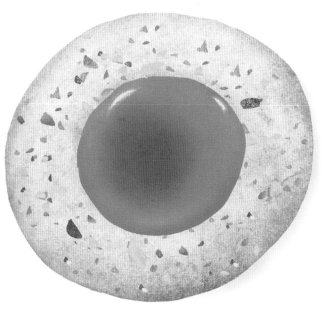

Preheat the oven to 180°C/160°C fan/Gas Mark 4 and line a large baking tray with baking paper.

Use an electric mixer to cream together the softened butter and sugar on a medium speed. Once light and fluffy, add in the vanilla extract and milk and mix in, then add the flour and salt and mix on a slow speed until it resembles a soft biscuit dough.

Tip the chopped pistachios into a small, separate bowl.

Use a dessertspoon to scoop out chunks of dough from the bowl, weigh them at about 45g each, and roll gently into balls between the palms of your hands. Tip each ball into the chopped pistachios, rolling them around until well coated, then place on the lined baking tray, spacing them 5cm apart.

Bake for 10 minutes, then remove from the oven and make a deep indent in the middle of each biscuit, pressing almost to the tray underneath (see tip). The indent should be about the size of a 50 pence piece.

Place the biscuits back in the oven for a further 10 minutes until golden brown all over.

Leave the biscuits to cool on the tray. Once cooled, fill the indent in each biscuit with a teaspoon of apricot jam.

TIP

Contrary to what the name suggests, we strongly recommend you *don't* use your thumb to make the indent in the middle of these biscuits. Mid-way through baking, they'll be as hot as the sun! We tend to use the back of a tablespoon-size measuring spoon, but the end of a wooden spoon or a wine-bottle cork will work well too.

ALLISON'S
Danish Snowball Biscuits

Allison, a former team member at Luminary, has been making these biscuits with her mum and grandma at Christmas time since she was small, but her family have been making them for generations. They would always agree to save some for Christmas morning, but if anyone couldn't resist pinching one, they would know from the tell-tale flurry of sugar 'snow' they left behind!

MAKES 30

115g unsalted butter, softened (you can substitute dairy-free margarine if you'd like to make these vegan or dairy free)

170g vegetable shortening (we use Trex), at room temperature
2 tsp vanilla extract
180g icing sugar
400g plain flour
1 tsp fine salt
125g walnuts, finely chopped

Using an electric mixer, mix together the butter, vegetable shortening and vanilla extract until smooth and fully combined. Add 100g of the icing sugar to the fats, a little at a time, and mix in.

Add the flour, salt and chopped walnuts and mix together to combine. Cover the bowl with clingfilm and refrigerate for 20–30 minutes.

Meanwhile, preheat the oven to 180°C/160°C fan/Gas Mark 4 and line a baking tray with baking paper. Use a dessertspoon to scoop out chunks of dough from the bowl, weigh them at about 30g each, and roll gently into balls between the palms of your hands. Place the balls on the lined baking tray, spacing them 5cm apart.

Bake for 20–25 minutes until the biscuits are golden brown and firm to a gentle touch. Remove from the oven and leave to cool on the tray for 3 minutes.

Tip the remaining 80g of icing sugar into a shallow bowl.

While the biscuits are still warm, roll each one in the bowl of icing sugar until well coated, then leave them to cool completely on a flat surface.

When completely cool, roll each biscuit in the icing sugar for a second time and sieve icing sugar over the top so that they are fully coated before serving.

NANNA'S AND MIM'S
Shortbread with an Espresso Twist

Some of the best recipes we know are family recipes – timeless classics, passed down from generation to generation, honed and refined by each new baker. Mim, a former baker at Luminary, was gifted a handwritten recipe book for her twenty-first birthday by her grandma, full to the brim with signature treats, such as this shortbread. Since then, Mim has fallen in love with our cafés' bespoke blend of espresso (courtesy of New Ground) and has used it to give her nanna's recipe an innovative new twist. It's a fantastic way to give a second life to leftover coffee grounds.

MAKES 10–15 BISCUITS

100g unsalted butter

10g freshly ground espresso (or leftover coffee grounds, pressed of excess water)

100g plain flour, plus extra for dusting

50g rice flour

50g caster sugar, plus extra (optional) to decorate

100g dark chocolate (optional), to decorate

Melt the butter in a saucepan over a gentle heat until completely melted, then add the espresso/coffee grounds to the pan and bring to a low simmer. Let your espresso and butter 'brew' for about 5 minutes, then remove from the heat. Leave the coffee-infused butter to cool to room temperature (no need to strain), then transfer to the fridge to set firm.

Cut the now-firm espresso butter into cubes.

Sift the flours into a large mixing bowl and add the caster sugar and the espresso butter cubes. Rub the butter into the flour (alternatively, use an electric mixer on a slow speed), mixing until the ingredients come together to form a ball of crumbly, speckled dough.

Wrap the dough in clingfilm and chill in the fridge for 30 minutes.

Meanwhile, preheat the oven to 150°C/130°C fan/Gas Mark 2 and line a large baking tray with baking paper.

Remove the dough from the fridge and gently roll out on a floured work surface to about 5mm thick. Use cookie cutters to cut out shapes and transfer these to the lined baking tray.

Gently prick each shortbread biscuit once with a fork.

Bake the shortbread for 35–40 minutes until pale golden brown.

You can either sprinkle the biscuits with a little caster sugar while they are still warm from the oven and leave to cool completely, or follow the instructions below to decorate with chocolate.

Place two-thirds of the chocolate in a small microwaveable bowl and melt it in the microwave, heating for 30 seconds at a time and stirring between each stage. When it has only just melted, tip in the remaining chocolate and stir until it's completely melted and shiny. This technique is a cheat's version of tempering called 'seeding' – it should give you shinier chocolate than just melting it all together.

Half-dip each shortbread biscuit into the chocolate, then leave to set on a sheet of greaseproof paper.

White Chocolate and Black Sesame Cookies

These are cookies of contrast – the earthy, bitter black sesame seeds are brought together with creamy, sweet white chocolate, creating a beautiful blend of taste and texture that we find irresistible.

MAKES 15 COOKIES

160g unsalted butter

40g caster sugar

130g soft light brown sugar

1 medium egg

1 tsp vanilla extract

40g glucose syrup (or golden syrup if you don't have any to hand)

250g plain flour

1 tsp bicarbonate of soda

½ tsp fine salt

30g cornflour

100g white chocolate chips or a bar cut into 1cm chunks (Milky Bar Buttons are particularly good in this recipe)

15g black sesame seeds

Melt the butter in the microwave (or in a small saucepan over a low heat) until liquid but not hot and spitting.

Using an electric mixer or whisk, mix the melted butter, caster sugar and brown sugar on a medium speed until they're well combined and the butter no longer separates. It should look rather like a thick caramel.

Add the egg, vanilla and glucose syrup (or golden syrup, if using) and beat until thoroughly mixed, scraping down the sides of the bowl with a spatula as needed.

In a small, separate bowl, weigh out the flour, bicarbonate of soda, salt and cornflour, then sift this over the egg mixture.

On a slower speed, mix the flour into the batter until it resembles a soft dough and there are no pockets of flour remaining. Tip in 80g of the white chocolate chips and stir gently into the dough. Don't over-mix once the chocolate chips are added or you'll get a tough cookie!

Tip the black sesame seeds into a small bowl or saucer and line a couple of large baking trays with baking paper.

Use a dessertspoon to scoop out chunks of cookie dough from the bowl, weigh them at about 50g each, and roll gently into balls between your hands. Lightly dip the top of each ball into the black sesame seeds and place, sesame-side up, on the lined baking trays, spacing them about 5cm apart. Stick 2–3 of the remaining white chocolate chips on the top of each ball. Place the trays of cookie balls in the fridge to chill for 20–30 minutes.

Meanwhile, preheat the oven to 180°C/160°C fan/ Gas Mark 4.

Bake for 8–10 minutes until the cookies have spread out and are golden around the edges but still slightly pale in the middle. Avoid the temptation to bake them until deep golden brown all over – they might look under-cooked in the middle, but will give you a gloriously chewy centre once they have cooled.

Leave the cookies to cool on the trays for 10 minutes before transferring to a wire rack to cool completely.

TIP

These cookies also bake perfectly, if not better, from frozen. This allows you to make a large batch in advance and bake them as and when you need (or bake a single cookie on one of *those* days, when an oven-warm cookie is the only cure). We recommend rolling them into balls and freezing in an airtight container for up to 3 months. When required, preheat the oven, pop them on a lined baking tray and bake for 10–12 minutes.

Malted Chocolate Biscuits

These are as fuss-free and fun to make as they are tasty. Using simple store-cupboard ingredients and requiring you to roll the dough into a long sausage, they're an entertaining baking activity to do with kids. If you can resist eating all the dough before it's baked, we're sure you'll love the malty milk-chocolate reward that comes out of the oven.

MAKES 24 SMALL BISCUITS

125g unsalted butter, softened
60g light brown sugar
125g plain flour
1 tsp baking powder
50g malted milk powder (we use Horlicks)
20g cocoa powder
a pinch of fine salt

Preheat the oven to 160°C/140°C fan/Gas Mark 3 and line a large baking tray with baking paper.

Cream together the softened butter and light brown sugar until pale and fluffy.

In a separate bowl, sift together the flour, baking powder, malted milk powder, cocoa and salt.

Gently mix the flour mixture into the butter mixture until a soft dough forms, being careful not to fling flour everywhere in the process!

Once a soft dough has formed, tip it out onto a clean work surface. Roll the dough into a long sausage, about 2cm thick and 1m long (or do it in sections, rolling a quarter of it at a time).

Using a sharp knife, cut the dough sausage into 24 even pieces, each 4cm long (during baking, these mini logs melt down to make rounded rectangular biscuits). Lift each piece onto the lined baking tray, spacing them 2cm apart.

Bake for 15–20 minutes until firm to the touch.

Leave to cool on the tray for 5 minutes before transferring to a wire rack to cool completely.

Vegan Chocolate and Sea Salt Cookies

When Mim joined us, she not only brought a wealth of cake-decorating experience and a kind and caring spirit, but a passion for making exquisite vegan bakes. Mim says this recipe is inspired by all the women she has worked with in the kitchen over the years – resilient, strong and incredible. Sprinkled lightly with sea salt, you'll savour every bite of these cookies!

MAKES 15

115ml olive oil
60ml cold water
210g soft light brown sugar
½ tsp vanilla extract
250g plain flour
30g cocoa powder
1 tsp baking powder
¾ tsp bicarbonate of soda
¼ tsp fine salt
175g vegan (70%) dark
   chocolate chips or a bar
   cut into 1cm chunks
   (check the packet to
   ensure it is dairy free)
flaky sea salt

Mix together the oil, water, sugar and vanilla until thoroughly combined and it looks like caramel.

In a separate bowl, sift together the flour, cocoa, baking powder, bicarbonate of soda and salt.

Tip the dry ingredients into the wet ingredients and mix to fully combine and create a soft dough.

Add the chocolate chips and mix until equally distributed. Cover the bowl with clingfilm and chill in the fridge for 30–60 minutes until firm.

Preheat the oven to 180°C/160°C fan/Gas Mark 4 and line 2 large baking trays with baking paper.

Use a dessertspoon to scoop out balls of dough onto the trays, spacing them 5cm apart to allow for spreading. Alternatively, weigh out balls of dough at 55g each, and roll them in your hands before placing on the trays. Top each cookie with a pinch of sea salt flakes.

Bake for 10–12 minutes until the cookies have firmed up around the edges.

Leave to cool on the trays for 5 minutes before transferring to a wire rack to cool completely.

TRAYBAKES

The sustenance of a homemade flapjack, the comfort of freshly baked brownies, the blissful indulgence of millionaire's shortbread... traybakes will always have a subtle familiarity and an ease for sharing. The aromas of the bakes you'll find in these pages have the ability to create an atmosphere of home. Ranging from sweet apples and warming spices,

to sharp lemon zest and buttery
shortbread, they'll fill your home
as you bake – an inviting welcome
to anyone who steps through the
door. These are everyday bakes
– they don't require a celebration
or special occasion, fancy equipment
or grand decoration. Instead, they're
treats to be shared and savoured
in life's little moments and on
everyday adventures.

GRACE'S STORY

The atmosphere of a supportive and comforting home is one that Luminary aims to create as we welcome apprentices like Grace to the bakery. This is her story.

After coming out of a refuge and being placed in a hostel, the overwhelming task of creating a new life stood in front of Grace. On her own, lacking family and support, Grace's main focus was providing for her daughter, Arya, and tackling the impending questions around basic necessities for provision. But when she came across Luminary's story in a magazine, she was reminded of her harboured dreams of becoming a pastry chef and knew that we had the potential to offer the support she was seeking and needing.

Grace's kind-hearted exuberance for a better life filled the rest of the women in her Luminary cohort with determination! Her enthusiasm for trying new ingredients and experimenting with flavours is why we called upon her as an apprentice to help create a new treat to be sold at Ben and Jerry's Scoop Shop in Soho. She began experimenting and until she made it absolutely perfect she wasn't going to give up – it took her nearly 20 tries to get it right. The result is on page 104.

Since graduating, Grace has returned to Luminary to work in the bakery. Her perseverance and boldness continues as she explores different ingredients and flavours, going above and beyond what is expected to create bakes of genius.

'No matter what happens at Luminary or with the apprentices, no matter what gets thrown at anyone, things will always be picked up and carried on. No one ever gives up! You'll always be able to look back – even if it's a month or a year – and see how much has changed. Nothing ever stays the same. There's always opportunity for growth – positive growth.'

GRACE'S
Honeycomb Cheesecake Blondies

For Arya

Grace explored many textures and tastes during the development of this recipe, but there was something that always drew her back to honeycomb – with its appeal of caramel, but lighter balance and crunchy twist. For Grace, this felt particularly nostalgic, reminding her of flavours she experienced as a child. It took her nearly 20 tries to get it right, but she persevered: 'There's something in perseverance that reminds me of Arya, my daughter – she's everything I love!' The resulting melt-in-the-mouth blondies were well worth it.

MAKES 12 GENEROUS SLICES

For the honeycomb
vegetable or sunflower oil, for greasing
50g caster sugar
25g golden syrup
½ tsp bicarbonate of soda

For the blondie batter
330g unsalted butter, melted, plus extra for greasing
3 medium eggs
330g soft light brown sugar
1 tsp vanilla extract
330g plain flour
1½ tsp bicarbonate of soda
½ tsp fine salt

For the cheesecake swirl
180g full-fat cream cheese
1 medium egg yolk
20g icing sugar
½ tsp vanilla extract

First, make the honeycomb. Line a deep baking tray with baking paper and smear with a little oil.

Tip the sugar and golden syrup into a deep saucepan and place over a low heat, swirling every now and again until all of the sugar has dissolved (you don't want it to bubble at this stage).

Once the sugar has melted, turn the heat up to medium, bring to a simmer and keep swirling for 2–5 minutes until it turns a deep amber colour. At this point, immediately take the pan off the heat and beat in the bicarbonate of soda with a spatula. It will start to foam and rise in the pan. Continue to mix for a few more seconds, then scrape the mixture out onto the oiled tray (be careful as the mixture will be very hot).

Leave it aside for at least 30 minutes – the honeycomb will continue to foam and grow and will eventually set rock hard.

Preheat the oven to 180°C/160°C fan/Gas Mark 4. Line the base of a 20 x 25cm baking tin with baking paper, greasing the sides with butter.

To make the blondie batter, melt the butter in the microwave or in a small saucepan over a low heat until liquid but not hot and spitting.

In a separate bowl, beat together the eggs, sugar and vanilla extract. Once the butter has melted, add it to the egg mixture and gently whisk until smooth and glossy.

In another small bowl, mix together the flour, bicarbonate of soda and salt. Tip this into the glossy mixture and mix until there are no pockets of flour remaining.

Break the honeycomb up into 2–3cm chunks and add to the blondie batter. Briefly stir through, then scrape it into the lined tin, spreading it flat.

In one final bowl, make the cheesecake swirl. Mix together the cream cheese, egg yolk, icing sugar and vanilla until smooth.

Dollop large blobs of the cheesecake mixture across the top of the blondie batter, then use a butter knife to swirl it into the batter to give a marbled effect on the top.

Bake for 40–45 minutes until golden brown all over but still a bit wobbly in the middle (the wobble is crucial, otherwise you'll have dry, cakey blondies). Once baked, leave to cool completely in the tins before cutting into 12 squares and tucking in!

IDA'S*

Honey and Walnut Drizzle Cake

Prior to her arrival at Luminary, Ida had been living in a safehouse after experiencing gender-based violence. English was not her first language and so she was shy at first, but very quickly her innovation with ingredients inspired us all. Coming from a disadvantaged background, Ida had to work hard at a very young age to put together the pieces she needed to complete a recipe – even churning her own butter. Although her family didn't have a lot of options, for Christmas and New Year they would always make *shendetlie*, one of the finest seasonal bakes in Albania and the inspiration behind Ida's traybake recipe. Every year, her family would look forward to this luxurious treat. With mouthwatering ingredients such as honey and walnuts enhancing the cake's flavour, it shouldn't be a surprise if you find people competing for the first taste!

MAKES 16 SLICES

For the cake
125g unsalted butter, melted,
    plus extra for greasing
2 medium eggs plus 1 yolk

125g caster sugar
200g runny honey
300g natural yoghurt
400g plain flour
2 tsp bicarbonate of soda
180g walnuts, finely chopped

For the syrup
275ml water
275g caster sugar
100g runny honey

*Name changed to protect identity

Preheat the oven to 180°C/ 160°C fan/Gas Mark 4. Grease a deep 20 x 25cm baking tin with a little butter and line the base with baking paper.

Combine the eggs, egg yolk and sugar in a large bowl and whisk together until pale, frothy and slightly thickened.

Whisk in the butter and honey, followed by the yoghurt.

Sift the flour and bicarbonate of soda over the mixture and stir in until no lumps of flour remain.

Fold the chopped walnuts into the batter and pour it into the prepared tin. Leave to rest for 10 minutes.

Bake in the oven for 45–50 minutes until dark golden brown and the sponge springs back to the touch. Set aside to cool in the tin.

While it cools, make the syrup. Combine the water, sugar and honey in a saucepan and bring to the boil. Reduce to a gentle simmer and cook for 15–20 minutes until it has reduced to a runny, slightly syrupy consistency.

Leaving the cake in the tin, use a sharp knife to cut the cake into diamonds, slicing it in intersecting diagonal lines, 5cm apart.

Pour the hot syrup over the cake and let it soak in for at least 30 minutes before serving, although it's even better if left to mature for a day.

RACHEL'S
Apple, Rosemary and Brown Butter Blondies

These blondies are the first thing that Rachel, our former Head Baker and trainer, baked for Alice and the team when she joined Luminary. They always take us back to those early days. We love the salty-sweet contrast in the blondie batter – the soft juicy apples, surrounded by comforting cinnamon and fresh rosemary. They're one of Rachel's favourite and most-baked recipes and everything we adore in one squidgy square!

MAKES 12

190g unsalted butter, plus
    extra for greasing
2 large eggs
100g soft dark brown sugar
100g soft light brown sugar
110g caster sugar
1½ tsp vanilla extract
175g plain flour
1 tsp baking powder
1 tsp fine salt
1½ tsp ground cinnamon
100g dark chocolate
    (70% cocoa solids),
    cut into chunks
2 eating apples (we use
    Granny Smiths), chopped
    into rough 1cm chunks
3 tsp finely chopped fresh
    rosemary (about 3 sprigs)

Preheat the oven to 180°C/160°C fan/Gas Mark 4 and grease and line a 20 x 25cm baking tin with a little butter and baking paper.

First, make your brown butter – also known as *buerre noisette*. Melt the butter in a small saucepan with a light-coloured base (if possible) over a gentle heat, then turn up the heat and let it bubble for 5–10 minutes. Watch it like a hawk – the milk solids can easily burn if left for too long. The butter will start to bubble and might spit a little – this is okay – then it will start to foam and you will be unable to see below the thick froth. Keep heating, swirling the pan from time to time, until it smells nutty and fragrant and the butter has turned an amber colour. Take it off the heat and pour into a large bowl, making sure you scrape the brown bits into the bowl as well – these are the cooked milk solids that have caramelised on the bottom of the pan and they give the butter its delicious nutty, caramel flavour. Set aside to cool for about 5 minutes.

Add the eggs, sugars and vanilla to the cooled butter and beat with an electric mixer for about 5 minutes until pale and thick.

Sift the flour, baking powder, salt and cinnamon over the top of the mixture and gently fold it in until no lumps of flour remain.

Finally, mix in the chopped chocolate, apple and rosemary. Pour the batter into the baking tin and smooth it out with a spatula.

Bake for 45–50 minutes until an inserted cocktail stick comes out clean. Unlike brownies, these blondies don't want a wobble in the middle, they should be reasonably firm when pressed.

Allow the blondies to cool completely in the tin before turning out and cutting into 12 pieces.

GRACE'S
Masala Chai and Berry Crumble Cake

The comforts of crumble cakes never cease to amaze. This was our exact reaction when Grace, one of our wonderful Luminary graduates, presented us with this cake while completing her apprenticeship in our bakery. Wow! Its bold chai influence came from two years of new discoveries with us after being disconnected from the world around her (after taking shelter in a refuge). One of those new discoveries was the chai latte, which inspired this far-too-tempting traybake recipe. It's the perfect early autumn bake, using the last of the summer fruits and comforting spices that hint towards the festive season ahead. It's a Sunday in your PJs, eating crumble and thinking 'everything is going to be fine' kind of cake.

MAKES 12 PIECES

For the sponge
150g unsalted butter, softened, plus extra for greasing
8 cardamom pods
1 tsp fennel seeds
10 black peppercorns
75ml whole milk
150g soft light brown sugar
3 medium eggs
175g self-raising flour
1 tsp ground cinnamon
½ tsp ground ginger
a pinch of ground cloves
1 tsp vanilla extract
150g frozen mixed berries

For the crumble topping
100g cold unsalted butter, cubed
150g plain flour
100g soft light brown sugar
a pinch of fine salt
100g frozen mixed berries

Preheat the oven to 180°C/160°C fan/Gas Mark 4 and grease and line a 20 x 25cm baking tin with baking paper.

Put the cardamom pods, fennel seeds and peppercorns into a pestle and mortar and bash to a spicy rubble. Alternatively, tip them into a plastic freezer bag and bash them with a rolling pin.

Tip the spice rubble into a small saucepan along with the milk and bring to a gentle simmer. As soon as it starts simmering, remove the pan from the heat and set aside to cool and stew.

In a large bowl, cream together the softened butter and sugar until light and fluffy (use an electric mixer if you have one). Tip in the eggs, one at a time, thoroughly beating in before adding the next.

Sift the flour, cinnamon, ginger and cloves over the mixture and fold in until no floury patches remain.

Strain the cooled spiced milk into the bowl through a fine sieve and stir into the batter along with the vanilla.

Finally, stir the frozen berries through the mixture and spoon it into the lined baking tin, spreading it out with a spatula.

Make the crumble topping by rubbing the cold butter into the flour with your fingertips until it resembles breadcrumbs. Stir the sugar and salt through the crumble until well combined.

Sprinkle the crumble topping across the top of the cake batter, followed by the berries.

Bake for 35–40 minutes until golden brown and an inserted skewer comes out clean. The cake should spring back to the touch.

Leave to cool completely in the tin, before cutting into 12 equal pieces.

MIMI'S

Cardamom Millionaire's Shortbread

Mimi is a skilled freelancer writer and a brilliant storyteller. She was a baker for Luminary between jobs and expert at giving her baking a creative twist, too. We love her take on a traditional millionaire's shortbread, with its crumbly cocoa base, cardamom vegan caramel and a glossy layer of dark chocolate – it's deliciously distinctive!

MAKES 12 PIECES

For the shortbread base
125g dairy-free baking
    margarine, softened (we
    use Stork's Baking Block)
40g caster sugar
185g plain flour
1 tsp cocoa powder
a pinch of fine salt

For the cardamom caramel
100g soft dark brown sugar
40ml water
20g dairy-free baking
    margarine
1 tsp ground cardamom
    (or the seeds from about
    8 large pods, ground
    in a pestle and mortar)
400ml coconut cream

For the chocolate topping
200g dark chocolate
    (70% cocoa solids),
    broken into pieces
25g coconut oil

Preheat the oven to 180°C/160°C fan/Gas Mark 4 and line a 20 x 25cm baking tin with baking paper.

Start with the shortbread base. Beat the margarine and sugar together in a bowl until light and fluffy, then gradually sift in the flour, cocoa powder and salt, beating it in until a soft, paste-like dough has formed. Tip the dough into the lined tin, pressing it down evenly over the base with your hands, and prick the surface all over with a fork.

Bake in the oven for 15–20 minutes until the shortbread looks dry on the top and is firm to the touch. Set aside to cool.

Meanwhile, make the caramel. Combine the sugar and water in a saucepan over a medium heat. Let the sugar dissolve and eventually turn to caramel. Don't stir! If you can't stand idly by and watch the caramel bubble into life, you can gently shake the pan a little.

After 5–6 minutes the caramel should be bubbling and caramelising. Once all the water has evaporated and the mixture is forming thick bubbles, whisk in the margarine and ground cardamom.

Pour in the coconut cream, whisking constantly to form a smooth, runny caramel. Turn the heat down to low and continue cooking for 20–30 minutes, whisking from time to time, until the caramel becomes noticeably thicker and darker. It's ready when it thickly coats the back of a spoon and sets thick when you dollop a little bit onto a cold plate.

Take the pan off the heat and pour the caramel over the cooled shortbread base. Use a spatula to spread it smoothly across the entire base and right into the corners. Leave to cool completely.

To make the chocolate topping, melt the chocolate and coconut oil together in a heatproof bowl set over a pan of simmering water (don't let the base of the bowl touch the water). Alternatively, gently melt them in the microwave, being careful to stop and stir the mixture every 30 seconds to avoid burning it.

Pour the smooth shiny chocolate topping over the cooled caramel and chill in the fridge for 1–2 hours until set.

Use a sharp knife to gently cut the traybake into 12 even slices. Try not to eat them all yourself – or at least not in one sitting!

TIP

This recipe calls for coconut cream – the thicker, creamier friend of tinned coconut milk. It's usually found in cartons in the Asian foods section of supermarkets. We wouldn't recommend using coconut milk instead, as it's a lot more watery and won't set the caramel.

Gingernut Tiffin with Crystallised Ginger

You can think of this tiffin as Rocky Road's older, more sophisticated sister. Laden with fiery crystallised ginger and crunchy gingernut biscuits, it's an indulgent treat to be taken seriously!

MAKES 20 SQUARES

300g dark chocolate
    (70% cocoa solids),
    broken into pieces
125g dairy-free baking
    margarine
50g golden syrup
½ tsp salt
350g gingernut biscuits
60g crystallised ginger,
    cut into 5mm pieces

Line a 20 x 25cm baking tin with baking paper.

Set a heatproof bowl over a pan of simmering water (don't let the base of the bowl touch the water). Add the chocolate, butter, golden syrup and salt to the bowl and let them melt together, slowly stirring from time to time.

Meanwhile, place the gingernuts in a plastic freezer bag and crush with a rolling pin until you have a mixture of larger pieces, crumbs and dust. Alternatively, briefly blitz them in a food processor.

Once the chocolate mixture has completely melted and is smooth and glossy, remove it from the heat. Tip in the gingernut rubble and crystallised ginger and stir until well combined.

Tip the chocolatey mixture into the lined tin and use the back of a spoon to gently press it into the tin, making sure to get right into the corners. Cover and chill in the fridge for 1–2 hours until set.

Once firm, cut into 20 equal squares.

RACHEL'S
Praline and Cream Brownies

Whether part of a celebration or a treat to mark the end of a long and hard day, moments of indulgence can make life lighter and that little bit sweeter. Fudgy with rich chocolate, caramel, silky cream cheese and toasted nuts, Rachel's brownies are as decadent as it gets!

MAKES 12

unsalted butter, for greasing
75g pecans

For the cream cheese swirl
225g cream cheese,
    at room temperature
1 medium egg yolk
75g caster sugar
a couple of drops of
    vanilla extract

For the caramel swirl
60g caster sugar
40g golden syrup
15g unsalted butter
40ml double cream

For the brownie batter
85g unsalted butter
100g dark chocolate
    (70% cocoa solids),
    broken into pieces
130g caster sugar

2 medium eggs
1 tsp vanilla extract
70g plain flour (gluten-free
    plain flour also works
    well here)
1½ tbsp cocoa powder
⅛ tsp fine salt

PRALINE AND CREAM BROWNIES

Preheat the oven to 180°C/160°C fan/Gas Mark 4. Line the base of a 20 x 25cm baking tin (or a slightly smaller one, if you'd like deeper brownies) with baking paper and grease the sides with butter.

Tip the pecans onto a baking tray and pop them into the oven for 10 minutes to toast. They'll start to smell fragrant when they're ready.

Meanwhile, make the cream cheese swirl. Beat together the cream cheese, egg yolk, sugar and vanilla until smooth and set aside.

To make the caramel swirl mixture, melt the sugar and golden syrup in a small, heavy-based pan over a low heat, swirling to dissolve all the sugar – do not stir! Turn the heat up to medium and continue to swirl the pan every now and again until you have a deep copper-coloured caramel. Reduce the heat to low, then gradually whisk the butter into the pan in small pieces, followed by the cream – it will spit a little to start with, so be careful! Once smooth and glossy, set aside to cool and firm up a little.

To make the brownie batter, melt the butter and chocolate together in a heatproof bowl set over a pan of simmering water (don't let the base of the bowl touch the water). Alternatively, gently melt them in the microwave, being careful to stop and stir the mixture every 30 seconds to avoid burning it.

Beat the sugar into the chocolate mixture, followed by the eggs and vanilla.

In a small, separate bowl, mix together the flour, cocoa powder and salt until it is completely combined and uniform in colour. Sift this into the brownie batter and mix in until the mixture is glossy and there are no more pockets of flour.

Break up the toasted pecans in your hands so you have some whole ones and some rubble, and stir half of them through the brownie batter. Pour the brownie batter into the lined tin and spread flat with a spatula. Dollop both the cream cheese and caramel swirl mixtures in about 8 blobs on top of the batter and swirl it in using a butter knife. Scatter the remaining pecans across the top and tap the baking tin on the worktop to flatten it all out.

Bake for 25–30 minutes until the middle has a little wobble but the edges feel firm (the wobble is crucial, otherwise you'll have dry brownies). Leave to cool completely in the tin. Cut into 12 squares.

MATILDA'S STORY

The pursuit of happiness is never far from most people's minds. For Matilda, it was a never-ending struggle, without the right to work. For seven years, it seemed as though time stood still for Matilda, until she received the news that she had been accepted into Luminary's programme. Then, hope began to rise.

Every single day, come rain or shine, Matilda made it to each training session. On one particular morning, she had fallen down the stairs and ended up in A&E. Even so, in typical Matilda style, she showed up to training in the afternoon on crutches!

After graduating from Luminary, Matilda went on to college, where she studied Level 3 Patisserie and Confectionery. We proudly celebrated with her as she graduated in 2020 with her certificate!

'It's not just baking – Luminary makes you feel at home, like family. We celebrate together! Everything everyone does means you're not alone. And I'm happy – baking makes me happy! I'm proud to say I am one of the Luminary girls!'

MATILDA'S
No-Bake 'Caramel' Nut Bars

Matilda's hope and courage spurred her on to create this amazing no-bake recipe for Luminary. They're a bold treat, full of fruity, nutty goodness and excellent as an afternoon pick-me-up!

MAKES 10 BARS

For the base
150g ground almonds
75g crunchy nut butter
    of your choice (we like
    peanut butter!)
50g coconut oil, melted
110g maple syrup

150g cornflakes (use gluten-
    free ones if required)

For the topping
15g coconut oil, melted
60ml warm water
70g dried dates (preferably
    Medjool), stoned and
    roughly chopped

70g dried apricots,
    roughly chopped
15g maple syrup
a pinch of salt

To decorate
100g chopped nuts
    of your choice

TIP
These nut bars work well with any nut butters or nuts you have in your cupboard.
We particularly like a peanut version using peanut butter and chopped peanuts.

Line a 900g/2lb loaf tin with baking paper.

First, make the base. In a food processor, blitz together the ground almonds, nut butter, coconut oil, maple syrup and cornflakes for a few minutes, until the mixture begins to hold together in a ball.

Press the sandy base mixture into the lined tin and chill in the fridge for 20–30 minutes.

Meanwhile, make the topping. Place all the topping ingredients in the cleaned food processor and blitz until smooth, scraping down the sides in between.

Spread the topping over the top of the chilled base, then sprinkle over the chopped nuts to decorate. Return to the fridge for a further 30 minutes.

Remove the slab from the tin and slice into 10 thin slices. Store the bars in the fridge for up to 5 days.

Cherry and Coconut Vegan Brownies

Luminary originally started as a wholesale bakery, supplying cafés with cakes and cookies. If you know where to look, you'll still find our bakes for sale in many cafés across London. These brownies are one of our stockists' favourites – loved by vegans and non-vegans alike – and with good reason: they're fudgy and rich, and bursting with juicy cherries and creamy coconut. You wouldn't believe they don't contain butter or eggs! They're perfect with a cup of coffee or warm from the tray.

MAKES 12

4 tsp (10g) ground flax seeds
60ml hot water
300g plain flour
300g soft light brown sugar
60g cocoa powder

40g desiccated coconut, plus extra to decorate
½ tsp salt
130g coconut oil
120g dark chocolate (70% cocoa solids), broken into pieces

1 tbsp lemon juice
1 tsp vanilla extract
170ml coconut milk drink (we use Alpro, see tip)
200g frozen pitted cherries (fresh are even better, just a bit more expensive)

TIPS
When flax seeds (also known as brown linseeds) are ground up and mixed with water, they form a gelatinous consistency that's perfect as an egg replacement and used here to bind the brownies together. You can find them pre-ground in most large supermarkets, usually in the health food section.

Any alternative milk will work in this recipe (almond, oat, soy...), but we love the added flavour that the coconut one brings.

Preheat the oven to 180°C/160°C fan/Gas mark 4. Line a 20 x 25cm baking tin with baking paper.

In a small bowl, mix together the ground flax seeds and hot water and set aside for about 10 minutes to thicken.

In a large bowl, mix together the flour, sugar, cocoa, desiccated coconut and salt until there are no lumps and it's uniform in colour.

Melt the coconut oil in a small saucepan over a low heat, then remove from the heat and tip in the chocolate. Stir the chocolate into the oil until all the chocolate is melted and the mixture is silky and smooth. If it hasn't all melted, return it to a gentle heat to warm through briefly.

Mix the lemon juice, vanilla extract, coconut milk drink and thickened flax-seed mixture into the chocolate-oil mixture.

Make a well in the middle of the dry ingredients, pour in the wet ingredients and mix until combined.

Spoon the batter into the lined tin and smooth out flat with a spatula.

Dot the top of the batter with the cherries, pressing them in slightly, and dust the top with a little extra desiccated coconut.

Bake for 20–25 minutes until set but still a little wobbly in the middle. Allow them to cool completely in the tin before cutting into 12 equal squares.

Lime Leaf Lemon Bars

Kaffir lime leaves are to South-East Asian cooks what bay leaves are to Western ones – they are often infused in soups, curries and stews to add background flavour. When finely chopped, they can be used in a similar way to lime zest. We love the more complex zing they bring to the top of our zesty lemon bars!

MAKES 12

For the shortbread base
265g plain flour
60g caster sugar
200g unsalted butter, melted

For the topping
zest of 2 lemons
265g caster sugar
65g plain flour
4 medium eggs
3 fresh kaffir lime leaves,
    stems removed, very
    finely chopped
160ml lemon juice (from
    2–3 large lemons)
icing sugar, for dusting

Preheat the oven to 190°C/170°C fan/Gas Mark 5 and line a 20 x 25cm baking tin with baking paper.

First, make the shortbread base. Mix together the flour and sugar in a large bowl, make a well in the middle and pour in the melted butter. Mix the butter into the flour until a ball of dough forms.

Tip the shortbread dough into the bottom of the lined tin and press down flat, working it into the corners. Prick the shortbread all over with a fork and bake in the oven for 20 minutes until golden around the edges.

While the base is cooking, make the topping. In a separate bowl, rub the lemon zest into the sugar to release its oils. Whisk the flour into the sugar, followed by the eggs and chopped lime leaves, then whisk in the lemon juice.

Remove the tin from the oven and pour the lemony mixture over the shortbread base. Carefully return to the oven for a further 15–20 minutes. Once baked, it should just have lost its wobble in the middle but it should not be firm to the touch.

Allow the bars to cool completely in the tin before placing in the fridge for 30–60 minutes to firm up. Once chilled, cut into 12 equal slices and dust the tops with icing sugar.

SMALL
CAKES

What the cakes in this chapter lack in size, they more than make up for in flavour, texture and beauty. As these small cakes are individually portioned and decorated, they make perfect picnic or party food – easy to share and more personal than a whole cake.

Muffins make eating cake for breakfast socially acceptable, cupcakes take away the stress of cutting a cake into even slices plus can be eaten almost anywhere, and friands and financiers are so delicate and pretty they'll have your friends and family cooing over what you've created.

MONICA'S STORY

Monica's passionate pursuit of a better life is the definition of tenacity. As a woman who had previously experienced years of violence against her, she struggled to find the confidence she needed to move forward. And as a single mother, she felt the weight of filling both parental shoes by herself. Despite the odds against her, she fought to regain stability and a better life for her child. After watching a friend graduate from Luminary's programme – and seeing its impact on her – Monica knew that she wanted to join the supportive community at the bakery, too.

Although she had always enjoyed cooking, baking remained a bit of an enigma to Monica. However, over the course of Luminary's programme, it became a passion – something that brought harmony to her soul. And being with women who believed in her gave her the determination she needed to keep going, even when circumstances were against her. When she broke her ankle, everyone pulled together to help, and she courageously came back and completed the programme!

'Because of my past, I wasn't able to believe in myself. Now, I'm with women who understand my background and who believe in me. The most important thing in life is strength. When you have it, no matter how many ups and downs, you still fight – you see power. That's what I see in Luminary – strength.'

Almond Butter and Banana Muffins

When Monica graduated, a version of these banana muffins were part of her application to work at Luminary as an apprentice. We couldn't possibly have turned her – or her delicious baking – down. And so, over time, she mastered the recipe and it took flight. We believe these are everything a banana muffin should be – moist, light and full of banana flavour. They are, quite simply, *impossible* to say 'no' to!

MAKES 12

100g whole almonds
150g plain flour
1 tsp ground cinnamon
1 tsp baking powder
1 tsp bicarbonate of soda

¼ tsp fine salt
80ml vegetable oil
60g soft dark brown sugar
1 tsp vanilla extract
65g natural yoghurt
75g almond butter
1 large egg

4 ripe bananas (approx. 400g when peeled – if large, just use 3 bananas)
20g Demerara sugar

TIP
To achieve the best flavour in your muffins, use really ripe bananas – bananas so brown and squishy you're unlikely to want to eat them raw, but will make excellent banana muffins.

Preheat the oven to 180°C/160°C fan/Gas Mark 4 and line a 12-hole muffin tin with paper muffin cases.

Spread the almonds out on a baking tray and toast in the oven for 10 minutes until fragrant. Set aside to cool before roughly chopping through them a few times to make almond 'shards'.

Sift the flour, cinnamon, baking powder, bicarbonate of soda and salt into a large bowl and mix until it is completely combined and uniform in colour.

In a separate bowl, whisk together the vegetable oil, sugar, vanilla, yoghurt, almond butter and egg until combined.

In a third bowl, mash the bananas until there are only a few small lumps, then whisk the bananas into the wet ingredients.

Make a well in the middle of the dry ingredients and pour the banana mixture into it. Gently stir the wet and dry ingredients together until there is no flour visible. Gently stir in half of the almonds, being careful not to over-mix the batter.

Evenly spoon the batter into the paper muffin cases and sprinkle the remaining almonds and Demerara sugar over the top.

Bake for 20 minutes until golden brown and an inserted skewer comes out clean. Leave to cool in the tin for 10 minutes before transferring to a wire rack to cool completely.

Sticky Fig Bran Muffins

Our Sticky Fig Bran Muffins are the ultimate mix between fibrous fuel for the day and cake for breakfast. They are sweet but wholesome, sticky but packed with wholegrains. They've kept our bakers going on their early morning shifts, and been a favourite post-workout snack for keen runners in our team.

MAKES 12

200g soft dark brown sugar
3 medium eggs
160ml vegetable or
    sunflower oil
250g natural yoghurt

grated zest and juice of
    ½ orange
200g bran flakes
150g wholemeal plain flour
1 tsp baking powder
1 tsp bicarbonate of soda
½ tsp fine salt

1 tsp ground cinnamon
½ tsp ground ginger
200g dried figs
a handful of rolled oats,
    for sprinkling

Preheat the oven to 170°C/150°C fan/Gas Mark 3 and line a 12-hole muffin tin with paper muffin cases.

Combine the sugar, eggs, oil, yoghurt, orange zest and juice in a large bowl and whisk together. Crush the bran flakes between your hands and add to the bowl, mixing to coat them well. Set aside for 10 minutes to soften.

In a separate bowl, sift together the flour, baking powder, bicarbonate of soda, salt, cinnamon and ginger and mix to combine.

Cut off and discard the hard stalk from the top of each fig and cut each one into small pieces, about 1–2cm.

Make a well in the middle of the dry ingredients, pour in the bran mixture and stir until you have a sloppy muffin batter with no pockets of flour remaining. Tip in the figs and stir them through.

Using an ice-cream scoop or dessertspoon, equally spoon the muffin batter between the paper cases – they will be quite full. Sprinkle a handful of oats across the top of each one.

Bake for 25 minutes until well risen and golden brown but still very slightly soft in the middle. Leave to cool in the tin for 5 minutes before transferring to a wire rack to cool completely.

Rye Chocolate Cupcakes with Orange Frosting

In our humble opinion, this is the *only* cupcake recipe you'll ever need. We were a bit speechless when Kate brought these cakes into the bakery a month or two into her internship, and convinced her to share the recipe with us. We've been making them for special occasions ever since, because they really are *very* special.

MAKES 12

For the cupcakes
125g white rye flour
1 tsp baking powder
½ tsp bicarbonate of soda
½ tsp fine salt
200g caster sugar
135ml vegetable oil
150ml buttermilk (you can
    use 100g natural yoghurt
    and 50ml milk, if you
    can't find buttermilk)

1 medium egg
1 tsp vanilla extract
60g cocoa powder
120ml boiling water

For the orange syrup and candied peel
½ orange
35g honey
70ml water
caster sugar, for dredging

For the frosting
50g cream cheese,
    at room temperature
100g unsalted butter,
    softened
250g icing sugar
1 tsp vanilla extract
2 tbsp orange syrup
    (see left and method)

Preheat the oven to 180°C/160°C fan/Gas Mark 4 and line a 12-hole muffin tin with paper muffin cases or large cupcake cases.

Sift together the flour, baking powder, bicarbonate of soda, salt and sugar in a large bowl.

In a separate bowl, whisk together the oil, buttermilk, egg and vanilla extract.

In a third small bowl, mix together the cocoa powder and boiling water until it forms a smooth paste. Whisk the chocolate paste into the wet ingredients.

Add the wet ingredients to the dry ingredients and slowly mix to incorporate – the mixture will be very runny. Evenly fill each paper case with the batter, filling each one no more than two-thirds full.

Bake for 15–20 minutes until the cakes spring back to the touch and an inserted skewer comes out clean. Leave to cool in the tin for 10–15 minutes before transferring to a wire rack to cool completely.

Meanwhile, make the orange syrup and candied peel. Use a vegetable peeler to pare the orange peel into thin strips of zest, avoiding as much of the white pith as possible. Place the peel in a small saucepan with the honey and water and set over a medium-low heat. Let it simmer for about 15 minutes, stirring occasionally, until you have a pale golden syrup. Strain the syrup from the peel, reserving both, and let cool to warm.

While still warm, cut the peel into long thin strips and toss in caster sugar until well coated. Shake off any excess sugar and set the candied peel on a tray to dry.

To make the frosting, place the cream cheese and butter in the bowl of a stand mixer fitted with the paddle attachment. Beat on medium speed for 1 minute until well combined. Add the icing sugar a spoonful at a time, mixing between additions. Once it is all combined, beat the frosting on a medium speed for a further 1 minute. Add the vanilla and orange syrup and beat again until just mixed in.

To decorate the cupcakes, place an ice-cream scoop of frosting directly in the centre of each cake. Take a butter knife and swipe it around the outside edge of the buttercream at a 45° angle to the cake, pushing the icing into a shallow mountain. Next, place the knife in the middle of the mound at a 45° angle and turn the cupcake one full turn in the other direction. This should create a nest-like shape of frosting. Decorate the tops with strips of the candied peel.

Smoky Toffee Apple Cakes

Toffee apples, cinnamon, smoky caramel... these cakes are like a firework display for your tastebuds! Decorated with satisfyingly sour physalis, their fallen-leaf-like casings are ripped open to reveal the bright orange fruit inside. Truly, nothing says 'autumn' like these. As soon as bonfire season is over, we're already counting down the months until we can start baking them again...

MAKES 12

115g cold unsalted butter, cubed, plus extra for greasing

225g self-raising flour, plus extra for dusting

2 tsp ground cinnamon

½ tsp fine salt

115g soft dark brown sugar

1 medium egg

100ml whole milk

1 tbsp black treacle

200g eating apples (we use 2–3 Braeburns or Granny Smiths), peeled, cored and chopped into 1cm pieces

75g raisins or sultanas

12 physalis, to decorate (see tip)

For the caramel

50ml whole milk

1 lapsang souchong tea bag

35g unsalted butter

30g soft light brown sugar

200g condensed milk

Preheat the oven to 180°C/160°C fan/Gas Mark 4. Grease the holes of a 12-hole muffin tin with butter, making sure to get into every corner and right up the sides, then dust with some flour, tipping it round the whole tin before shaking any excess out.

Sift the flour, ground cinnamon and salt into a large bowl and mix together. Tip in the cold cubed butter and, using your fingertips, rub the butter into the flour until it looks coarse and sandy, with no large lumps of butter visible. Stir in the dark brown sugar, breaking it up if it's lumpy.

In a separate bowl or jug, whisk together the egg, milk and treacle until combined.

Make a well in the middle of the dry ingredients, pour in the wet ingredients and mix to form a stiff

---

TIP

Physalis are also known as cape gooseberries and are available in most supermarkets. They give a great sharp-sour contrast to the sweetness of the caramel. If you can't find them, slices of fresh fig or blackberries are also lovely here.

---

batter. Add the chopped apple and raisins or sultanas to the bowl and mix through until just combined.

Evenly distribute the batter between the holes of the prepared muffin tin and smooth flat with the back of a teaspoon. Bake for 15–20 minutes until the cakes spring back when lightly pressed and are golden brown.

Leave to cool in the tin for 5 minutes, then turn the tin upside down on a clean work surface and shake a little so the cakes fall from the tin. Place them bottoms up on a wire rack to cool completely.

To make the caramel, add the milk and tea bag to a small saucepan and bring to the boil. Simmer for 1 minute, then remove and discard the tea bag. Add the butter and light brown sugar to the milk and stir over a medium heat until melted and combined. Stir in the condensed milk and bring back to the boil, stirring constantly to avoid it sticking and burning on the bottom of the pan. Keep heating and stirring until the caramel becomes a deep golden brown colour. Leave to cool slightly for 5 minutes.

Carefully spoon the warm caramel over the top of each cake, letting it drip down the sides of each one, then leave to cool.

Once the caramel has cooled, rip the paper-like cases of the physalis so that they're fully open and press into the caramel on top of each cake.

Lemon and Earl Grey Friands

Delicately aromatic and deliciously fragrant, our lemon friands found their perfect partner in Earl Grey tea. In this original Luminary recipe from years gone by, we use the tea leaves to infuse the butter before baking them into the almond cake mixture. The leaves release their subtle flavour and bergamot oils and give the finished friands an attractive speckle.

MAKES 12

200g unsalted butter, plus extra for greasing
gluten-free or plain flour, for dusting
1 Earl Grey tea bag, ripped open (see tip)

250g icing sugar
½ tsp fine salt
200g ground almonds
6 medium egg whites
finely grated zest of 1 medium lemon
30g flaked almonds

To decorate
3 tbsp lemon curd
1 tbsp hot water
dried blue cornflower petals (optional)
extra Earl Grey tea leaves (optional)

Preheat the oven to 200°C/180°C fan/Gas Mark 6. Grease the holes of a 12-hole muffin tin with butter, making sure to get into every corner and right up the sides, then dust with some flour, tipping it round the whole tin before shaking any excess out.

In a small saucepan, melt the butter with the tea leaves, then set aside to cool.

Sift the icing sugar, salt and ground almonds into a bowl and mix together.

In a separate large bowl, use an electric whisk to whisk the egg whites to soft peaks (when you lift the whisk out, it creates peaks in the egg mixture that slowly fall back into the bowl).

Tip the dry ingredients and lemon zest into the bowl of egg whites and gently fold in with a spatula, then pour in the cooled butter and fold in to form a light and bubbly batter.

Equally spoon the friand batter between the holes of the muffin tin and smooth the tops with the back of a teaspoon. Sprinkle the flaked almonds over the top of each one.

Bake for 20–25 minutes until the middles are just firm to the touch and the tops are beautifully golden. Leave them to cool completely in the tin before carefully turning out onto a wire rack or plate.

To decorate, gently warm the lemon curd and hot water in the microwave or in a small saucepan until runny and bubbling. Brush the mixture over the top of each friand and sprinkle with dried blue cornflower petals and a few more tea leaves, if you like.

TIP

Use a tea bag with finely ground leaves, not coarse or loose-leaf tea.
The tea is mixed into the friand batter, so larger leaves
can be woody and unpleasant to eat.

GRACE'S
Rye, Pear and Cardamom Financiers with Pistachios

As a child, Grace never had the freedom to explore bakeries, even though she was drawn to them. As time passed, her desire for a career in baking did not subside, but disadvantage began to paralyse her life from moving forward. It wasn't until she embarked on an apprenticeship with Luminary that her dream began to come true. After graduating, Grace took a job at a sourdough bakery, immersing herself in the world of grains and spices. Cardamom, in particular, piqued her interest and inspired her to create these delicate cakes, fit for afternoon tea or dessert. Their complex taste and aesthetic beauty are worth the small extra effort they take to make!

MAKES 10

120g unsalted butter, cubed,
    plus extra for greasing
95g wholegrain or
    dark rye flour, plus
    extra for dusting
3 firm Conference pears
6 cardamom pods,
    crushed but not ground

220g icing sugar
1 tsp baking powder
½ tsp fine salt
75g ground almonds
100g unsalted pistachios,
    finely chopped
220g egg whites
    (about 6 large eggs)

To serve
250g full-fat crème fraîche
½ tsp vanilla extract
25g unsalted pistachios,
    finely chopped

Preheat the oven to 200°C/180°C fan/Gas Mark 6. Grease 10 holes of a muffin tin with butter, making sure to get into every corner and right up the sides, then dust with some flour, tipping it round the tin before shaking any excess out.

Place the pears on a baking tray and bake in the oven for 10–20 minutes. They should be slightly soft but still firm when squeezed. Once baked, set them aside to cool completely.

Place the butter and cardamom pods in a saucepan over a medium heat. Cook, swirling occasionally, until the butter is browned (see browning butter method on page 108). Set aside to cool slightly.

In a medium bowl, sift together the icing sugar, rye flour, baking powder, salt and ground almonds. Add the finely chopped pistachios and stir in.

In a separate bowl, gently froth the egg whites with a whisk until bubbles appear and they are loosened. You don't want to whip them or try to make a foam. Add the loosened egg whites to the dry ingredients and mix until smooth.

Strain the butter to remove the cardamom and check the temperature – the butter should be warmer than room temperature but not so hot that it cooks the egg. Pour the strained butter in a stream into the batter, mixing as you do so, until the batter is smooth and glossy. Cover the bowl and chill in the fridge for at least 1 hour.

While the batter is resting, quarter and core the cooled pears. Gently cut 4–5 thin slices along each quarter, but keep them all attached at the top to make a fan shape. Also, bring the oven back up to temperature.

Once the batter has rested, spoon it into each muffin hole, filling them three-quarters full. Gently lay a pear fan over the top of each one (you might need to trim them to fit) and bake in the oven for 20–25 minutes until golden and a skewer inserted into the centre comes out clean.

To serve, mix the crème fraîche with the vanilla and gently spoon a dollop onto one side of the top of the cooled financiers. Sprinkle over the chopped pistachios to decorate.

Blackcurrant, Lavender and Mascarpone Cakes

In the days when we had a seasonal cake of the month, this one always belonged to July – the season of blackcurrants and lavender, both flavours evocative of English summertime. Since fresh blackcurrants can be hard to come by (and not everyone has a lavender bush growing nearby), we've made the recipe easy to bake all year round. Tart blackcurrant jam gives purple ripples to the almond sponge and we use dried lavender buds for their delicate perfume.

MAKES 12

150g unsalted butter, softened, plus extra for greasing
gluten-free or plain flour, for dusting
150g caster sugar
¾ tsp dried lavender buds

3 medium eggs
300g ground almonds
1 tsp vanilla extract
100g blackcurrant jam (preferably one with real pieces of blackcurrant in it)

For the mascarpone icing
120g mascarpone cheese, at room temperature
20g icing sugar
¼ tsp vanilla bean paste

To decorate
3 tbsp blackcurrant jam
a few dried lavender buds

Preheat the oven to 180°C/160°C fan/Gas Mark 4. Grease the holes of a 12-hole muffin tin with butter, making sure to get into every corner and right up the sides, then dust with some flour, tipping it round the whole tin before shaking any excess out.

In a large bowl or with an electric mixer on a medium speed, cream together the butter, sugar and lavender buds for about 5 minutes until fluffy and pale in colour. Beat in the eggs, followed by the ground almonds and vanilla extract. Fold the blackcurrant jam through the mixture so that it's loosely rippled through but far from a uniform purple colour.

Divide the cake batter equally between the holes of the muffin tin, smoothing out the tops with the back of a teaspoon. Bake for 20 minutes, or until an inserted cocktail stick comes out clean and they are golden brown and firm to the touch.

Leave the cakes to cool in the tin for 5 minutes before tipping the tin upside down and gently shaking the cakes out onto a wire rack to cool completely. You may need to carefully run a knife around the edge of each cake if they're a little stuck, but try to avoid this if possible.

To make the mascarpone icing, mix together the mascarpone cheese and icing sugar, followed by the vanilla bean paste, to give you a smooth, silky, speckled icing.

Once the cakes are cool, pipe (or spoon, if you don't have a piping bag) a little 'kiss' of the icing on the top of each upturned cake, slightly off-centre, then top with a little spoonful of blackcurrant jam and a small sprinkling of lavender buds.

Honey and Camomile Cakes

The camomile tea used in these cakes is made from dried flower heads, so it's delightfully floral and an excellent companion to honey. The cakes are so light and delicate, 'fairy cakes' might have been a better name for them!

MAKES 12

75g cold unsalted butter, cubed, plus extra for greasing
180g plain flour, plus extra for dusting
200g granulated sugar
1½ tsp baking powder
¾ tsp bicarbonate of soda
a pinch of fine salt

2 camomile tea bags, ripped open (see tip)
160ml whole milk
1 large egg
1 tsp vanilla extract

For the syrup
2 tbsp honey
3 tsp boiling water
1 camomile tea bag

To decorate (optional)
dried or fresh camomile flowers and finely grated lemon zest

TIP
Use a tea bag with finely ground leaves, not coarse or loose-leaf tea. The tea is mixed into the cake batter, so larger leaves can be woody and unpleasant to eat.

Preheat the oven to 180°C/160°C fan/Gas Mark 4. Grease the holes of a 12-hole muffin tin with butter, making sure to get into every corner and right up the sides, then dust with some flour, tipping it round the whole tin before shaking any excess out.

Sift the flour, sugar, baking powder, bicarbonate of soda, salt and the contents of the camomile tea bags into a large bowl and mix together. Tip in the cold cubed butter and, using your fingertips, rub the butter into the flour until it looks coarse and sandy, with no large lumps of butter visible.

In a separate bowl or jug, whisk together the milk, egg and vanilla.

Make a well in the middle of the dry ingredients, pour in half of the wet ingredients and whisk in until just incorporated. Add the second half and continue to whisk until no flour or lumps remain.

Divide the batter between the muffin holes using an ice-cream scoop or large spoon. Bake for 18–20 minutes, or until the cakes spring back when lightly touched.

Leave the cakes to cool in the tin for 5 minutes before tipping them out onto a wire rack to cool completely.

To make the syrup, mix together the honey, boiling water and the tea bag in a small bowl and leave to steep for 5 minutes. Squeeze out the tea bag with the back of a spoon and remove from the syrup.

Prick the top of the cakes all over with a small skewer. Using a teaspoon, spoon the camomile syrup over the cakes and leave it to soak in. If wished, decorate each cake with a sprinkling of dried or fresh camomile flowers and some lemon zest.

WHOLE CAKES

A freshly baked cake is one of the simplest and greatest pleasures in life. They often accompany grand moments of celebration or a quiet moment of indulgence. Our bakers take such care to create eye-catching celebration cakes for special occasions and to mark memorable moments. We love to use fresh fruit, herbs and spices to construct visually stunning centrepieces that reflect the delectable flavours inside each cake. They're (almost) too beautiful to cut into!

But cakes don't always have to accompany a party. Some of our favourites are the kind you'd enjoy making (and then promptly eating) on a drizzly afternoon, just to delight in the process, or to share with friends over a cup of tea. Cakes, whether you're baking or eating them, provide moments to cherish.

GISELLE'S STORY

The therapeutic nature of baking cakes can be a pleasure in itself and is something that brought Giselle hope amidst disadvantage.

Life prior to prison was a battle for Giselle. She had been living on the streets and risking everything to make ends meet. When she was released, she was determined to turn her life around. She had so much to live for and didn't want to let another day go by where her circumstances restricted her ambition for a better tomorrow. After being introduced to Luminary by a recruitment consultancy charity working with ex-offenders, she was finally ready to let her ambition loose.

Embracing the Luminary experience opened Giselle's eyes to new opportunities, drawing out skills that were yet to be explored. The art of preparing food for others is strong within Giselle's heritage – with a baker for a grandad and talented cooks for parents, culinary creativity is in her blood. Similarly, being of Jamaican, Malaysian and Irish descent, she embraces her international origins by bringing together flavours and different traditional cultural dishes from around the world.

Luminary has now become a home for Giselle – a network of women supporting each other.

'We all feel that the issues we're facing are the biggest or hardest thing we've ever had to deal with. Then, I met some of the amazing women coming through Luminary and it put things into perspective. They've all come from such extraordinary struggles and the most inspirational factor among these women is strength of character and perseverance. They are a constant reminder to me that we are all warriors.'

GISELLE'S
Lemon and Poppyseed Cotton Cake

Inspired by a Japanese vanilla cake, Giselle adapted this recipe so that the clean and light flavour of lemon complements its delicacy. 'Heavenly' is the only word to describe it. Whether a simple indulgence or to mark a moment of celebration, this cake aims to please – pair it with a cup of Earl Grey.

SERVES 8–10

unsalted butter, for greasing
4 medium eggs
80g white granulated sugar
1½ tsp lemon extract
finely grated zest of 1 large
    lemon (or 2 small) and
    a squeeze of the juice
65ml vegetable oil
70ml whole milk
    (or a dairy-free milk,
    such as oat or almond)
120g plain flour
1 tsp baking powder
30g poppyseeds
icing sugar, for dusting

Preheat the oven to 160°C/140°C fan/Gas Mark 3. Grease and line the base and sides of a 20cm cake tin (not a loose-bottomed one) with baking paper, ensuring the strip around the side reaches at least 5cm above the top of the tin. Wrap the outside of the tin with foil.

Separate the egg yolks from the whites, placing the yolks in a medium mixing bowl and the egg whites in a large grease-free mixing bowl.

Whisk the egg yolks with half of the sugar until pale and light. Add the lemon extract, lemon zest, oil and milk and gently stir to combine. Sift the flour and baking powder over the mixture and mix until just combined, being careful not to over-mix.

Whisk the egg whites with the squeeze of lemon juice and the remaining sugar until it forms stiff peaks when the beaters are lifted sharply out of the bowl. This should take around 5 minutes with an electric whisk.

Gently fold half of the egg whites and all of the poppyseeds into the batter, then pour the batter into the remaining egg whites, scraping down the sides of the bowl. Gently fold and mix until there are no lumps of egg whites left, being careful not to knock out too much air.

Spoon the mixture into the prepared tin and gently spread flat.
Place the tin into a water bath (fill a roasting tray with enough
boiling water to reach three-quarters of the way up the sides of the
tin). Bake for 25 minutes, then turn the oven up to 180°C/160°C fan/
Gas Mark 4 and bake for a final 10 minutes.

Once baked, carefully remove the tin from its water bath and bang
the tin sharply on the work surface a couple of times (this will help
prevent the cake shrinking). Allow the cake to cool in the tin for
30 minutes before turning out onto a serving plate.

Lightly dust the top with icing sugar to serve.

Pear and Saffron Upside-Down Cake

There's something nostalgic and heart-warming, about an upside-down cake. A custard-yellow sponge sitting atop – or rather underneath – syrupy pineapple rings. And occasionally, if you're lucky, a couple of glacé cherries. It's often reminiscent of simpler times, of the seventies and school lunches. Our modern version, with saffron and sliced pears, is better suited to a dinner party than the dinner hall, but contains all the same comforting nostalgia that we often crave.

SERVES 6–8

100g unsalted butter,
    softened, plus extra
    for greasing
400g tin of pear halves
100g plain flour
1 tsp baking powder
½ tsp bicarbonate of soda
a pinch of fine salt
100g caster sugar
2 medium eggs
1 tsp vanilla extract
vanilla ice cream or custard,
    to serve

For the caramel
50g caster sugar
50g unsalted butter
6 threads of saffron

Preheat the oven to 200°C/180°C fan/Gas Mark 6. Grease and line the base of a deep 20cm cake tin with baking paper (don't use a loose-bottomed tin, as the syrup will seep out).

Start with the caramel. Place the sugar in a small saucepan and cook over a low heat until it has melted. Don't stir, only swirl the pan until it turns golden brown. Stir in the butter and saffron threads, then pour into the base of the prepared cake tin.

Drain the tin of pear halves, reserving the juice for later. Cut each pear half into slices and neatly arrange them on top of the caramel, overlapping them slightly.

In a small bowl, mix together the flour, baking powder, bicarbonate of soda and salt.

In a separate bowl, cream together the butter and sugar until light and fluffy. Beat the eggs in, one at a time, followed by the vanilla extract, flour mixture and 3 tablespoons of the tinned pear juice. Pour the batter over the top of the pears in the tin.

Bake for 30–35 minutes until golden brown on top and the sponge springs back to the touch.

Leave to cool in the tin for 5 minutes, then loosen the cake from the sides with a knife and turn upside-down onto a serving plate. Peel off the paper and serve warm with ice cream or custard.

HENRIETTA'S
Plum and Ginger Pudding Cake

As a Luminary Bakery ambassador, Henrietta Inman has passed her baking knowledge and skills on to many of our trainees, especially on how to use natural ingredients, seasonal produce and wholefoods. This cake is a great example of what we love about Hen's baking – delicious, beautiful and full of goodness. Lifted by fresh plums that sink into the moist cake, the wholegrain flour and earthy rapeseed oil add an extra depth of flavour and the yoghurt makes it super soft, coming together to create that perfect sticky ginger cake that we'll never tire of.

SERVES 8–10

110ml rapeseed oil, plus extra for greasing
180g wholegrain or white spelt flour
½ tsp ground cinnamon

80g Demerara sugar
180g molasses sugar (or dark brown muscovado or soft dark brown sugar)
2 large eggs
80g natural yoghurt

90g fresh root ginger, very finely grated (see tip)
4 tsp boiling water
1 tsp bicarbonate of soda
450g plums (buying weight), halved and stoned

TIP
For a good ginger flavour you need all the juices and stringy bits that will come from grating the piece of ginger – don't throw any of that away!

Preheat the oven to 160°C/140°C fan/Gas Mark 3. Grease and line the base of a deep 20cm cake tin with baking paper (don't use a loose-bottomed tin as the cake mix is quite runny and will leak out).

In a large bowl, sift together the flour and ground cinnamon to get rid of any lumps.

In a separate bowl, use a whisk to thoroughly mix together the rapeseed oil, sugars, eggs, yoghurt and ginger.

Make a well in the centre of the flour mixture, pour in the wet ingredients and gradually mix it in to form a runny batter.

In a separate bowl or jug, combine the boiling water with the bicarbonate of soda. Add this to the mixture, folding it in gently, until everything is well combined and there are no more pockets of flour visible.

Pour the batter into the prepared tin. Arrange the plum halves on top, overlapping them if necessary and letting them sink into the batter.

Bake for 65–75 minutes, turning the tin around in the oven halfway through. The cake is ready when the top springs back to the touch and a skewer inserted into the centre comes out clean with a just few crumbs clinging to it.

Leave to cool in the tin for 30 minutes, then remove from the tin and enjoy when it's still a little warm. The cake will keep well in the fridge for up to 5 days.

Raspberry and Redcurrant Buttermilk Layer Cake

We like to think of berries as the jewels of the natural world and love how they adorn this layer cake like a crown. The tartness of the buttermilk, raspberries and redcurrants in the pillowy sponge offsets the sweetness of the buttercream and brings a beautiful pop of colour with every slice. Reminiscent of a beloved Victoria Sponge, it really is a cake fit for royalty – or that someone special in your life!

SERVES 10–12

345g unsalted butter,
    softened, plus extra
    for greasing
420g plain flour, plus extra
    for dusting
1 tsp fine salt
1 tsp baking powder
1 tsp bicarbonate of soda
400g caster sugar
3 medium eggs, plus
    2 egg whites
2 tsp vanilla extract
200ml buttermilk
    (alternatively, mix
    60ml whole milk with
    140g natural yoghurt)
150g fresh raspberries
150g redcurrants

For the buttercream
300g unsalted butter,
    softened
625g icing sugar
70ml buttermilk
    (alternatively, mix
    20ml whole milk with
    50g natural yoghurt)
1 tsp vanilla extract
a pinch of fine salt

For the filling
100g raspberry jam
100g redcurrant jelly

To decorate (optional)
freeze-dried raspberry
    powder or pieces
fresh raspberries
fresh redcurrants
coconut shavings
dried rose petals
pomegranate seeds
sprigs of fresh rosemary

Preheat the oven to 180°C/160°C fan/Gas Mark 4. Grease and line three 20cm cake tins with baking paper. Dust the greased edges of the tins with a little flour, tapping out any excess.

Sift the flour, salt, baking powder and bicarbonate of soda into a bowl and mix together.

In a separate large bowl, use an electric mixer to cream together the butter and caster sugar until light and fluffy. Beat in the eggs, egg whites and vanilla extract (it will look a little separated, but don't worry – it will come back together once the flour has been added). Gently mix in the flour, followed by the buttermilk and mix until there are no lumps left.

Fold the raspberries and redcurrants into the batter and evenly spoon it into the cake tins, smoothing the tops out with a spatula. Bake in the oven for 25–30 minutes until the sponges spring back to the touch and an inserted skewer comes out clean.

Leave the sponges to cool in the tins for 5 minutes, before turning out onto wire racks to cool completely.

Meanwhile, make the buttercream. In a large bowl, beat the butter until soft, then gradually add half of the icing sugar, a spoonful at a time, beating it in between each addition. Mix in the buttermilk, vanilla and salt, then beat in the other half of the icing sugar.

In another small bowl, stir together the raspberry jam and redcurrant jelly to loosen and combine them.

When the sponges are completely cool, trim the domed tops off with a bread knife to make them flat. Reserve the cake you trimmed off and crumble it onto a baking tray. Bake the cake crumbs in the oven at 180°C/160°C fan/Gas Mark 4 for 5–10 minutes until crisp.

Place a cake board or serving plate on a turntable or work surface (see tip on page 163) and smear a little buttercream on the top. This buttercream will act as 'glue' and stop the cake from sliding around. Peel off the baking paper from the sponge layers and place the first sponge layer, cut-side up, on the cake board or plate. Spread a quarter of the buttercream on the top of the sponge, going right to the edge. Leave an indent in the middle of the buttercream and fill it with half of the jam filling, spreading it to about 2cm away from the edge of the cake.

RASPBERRY AND REDCURRANT BUTTERMILK LAYER CAKE

Place a second sponge layer on top of the buttercream, cut-side down. Spread another quarter of the buttercream on the top of this second layer, pushing it just over the edge, followed by the remaining jam filling.

Place the third sponge layer on top, cut-side down. Spread another quarter of the buttercream on the top of this layer, pushing it just over the edge.

Spread the final quarter of the buttercream around the sides of the cake, until the whole cake is covered in an even layer of buttercream and any gaps are filled. Place a bench scraper at a 90-degree angle against the side of the cake (see tip, below) and turn the turntable (or your plate) to smooth the sides flat and create a patchy or 'naked' look to the icing on the sides of the cake. (Don't worry if you push some buttercream onto the top of the cake).

To finish the cake with a smooth, 90-degree angle on the top, use a palette knife to neatly drag the top edge of buttercream into the middle of the cake.

To decorate, mark out a Luminary crescent moon shape on the top of the cake using freeze-dried raspberry powder, tapering off the ends – this will be your guide for the rest of the toppings. Place chunks of the baked cake crumble at intervals around the crescent shape, with the largest pieces at the widest section of the moon and smaller pieces towards the ends. Repeat with the raspberries and redcurrants, draping them across the top. Finally, place the coconut pieces, rose petals, pomegranate seeds and rosemary sprigs in among the fruit, spacing them evenly and keeping the ends of the moon shape tapered.

TIP

At Luminary, we use a few of bits of equipment only keen cake makers usually own: a turntable, a small palette knife and a bench scraper. They make getting a perfectly smooth finish on a cake a lot easier and are well worth the investment if you decorate cakes regularly. If you don't have these to hand, instead of a turntable, you can place the cake on a large, flat plate and rotate it on your work surface. A butter knife and spatula are sufficient instead of a palette knife. And don't worry about the bench scraper – you'll be fine without!

Spiced Squash Layer Cake with Cream Cheese Icing

This recipe reminds us of the seasons changing, as the leaves turn from green to gold and a new chill is found in the air. The smell of roasting squash and pumpkin spice in this cake will rise from the oven and fill your kitchen as you bake, in a glorious celebration of harvest time. Topped with fluffy cream cheese icing and a sprinkling of pumpkin seeds, it's hard to imagine a better way to celebrate autumn!

SERVES 10–12

1 medium butternut squash
   (about 750g pre-peeled
   buying weight)
unsalted butter, softened,
   for greasing
450g self-raising flour, plus
   extra for dusting
300g soft light brown sugar
120g black treacle
50g natural yoghurt
240ml vegetable oil
1 tsp vanilla extract
4 medium eggs
½ tsp fine salt
1 tsp bicarbonate of soda
2 tsp ground ginger
2 tsp ground cinnamon
1 tsp ground nutmeg

For the icing

200g unsalted butter,
   softened
100g cream cheese,
   at room temperature
300g icing sugar
1 tsp vanilla extract

To decorate (optional)

¼ tsp ground cinnamon
5–6 physalis (also known as
   cape gooseberries)
sprigs of fresh rosemary
pumpkin seeds
unsalted pistachios, shelled

Preheat the oven to 180°C/160°C fan/Gas Mark 4 and line a baking tray with baking paper.

Cut the butternut squash in half, scoop out the seeds and score the flesh, going as deep as the skin. Place the halves upside-down on the prepared tray, cover with foil and bake for 1 hour until soft to the tip of a knife. Leave to cool, uncovered.

Meanwhile, grease and line the base of three 20cm cake tins with baking paper. Dust the greased inside edges of the tins with a little flour, tapping out any excess.

In a large bowl, whisk together the brown sugar, treacle, yoghurt, oil, vanilla and eggs until well combined.

Peel the skin off the cooled squash and weigh out 450g of the flesh. Mash until smooth with a potato masher or whiz in a blender to a purée. Scrape the squash purée into the egg mixture and whisk in. Sift the flour, salt, bicarbonate of soda and ground spices over the mixture and fold in until no lumps remain.

Evenly pour the batter into the prepared tins, then bake for 20–25 minutes until the sponges spring back to the touch and an inserted skewer comes out clean.

Leave the sponges to cool in the tins for 5 minutes, before turning out onto a wire rack to cool completely.

Meanwhile, make the icing. In a large bowl, beat the butter and cream cheese together until fluffy and glossy. Gradually beat in the icing sugar, a spoonful at a time, followed by the vanilla.

When the sponges are completely cool, trim the domed tops off with a bread knife to make them flat. Reserve the cake you trimmed off and crumble it onto a baking tray. Bake the cake crumbs in the oven at 180°C/160°C fan/Gas Mark 4 for 5–10 minutes until crisp.

Place a cake board or serving plate on a turntable or work surface (see tip on page 163) and smear a little icing on the top. This icing will act as 'glue' and stop the cake from sliding around. Peel off the baking paper from the sponge layers and place the first sponge layer, cut-side up, on the cake board or plate. Spread a quarter of the icing on the top of the sponge, pushing it just over the edge.

Place a second sponge layer on top of the icing, cut-side down. Spread another quarter of the icing on the top of this second layer, pushing it just over the edge.

SPICED SQUASH LAYER CAKE WITH CREAM CHEESE ICING

Place the third sponge layer on top, cut-side down. Spread another quarter of the icing on the top of this layer, pushing it just over the edge.

Spread the final quarter of the icing around the sides of the cake, until the whole cake is covered in an even layer of icing and any gaps are filled. Place a bench scraper at a 90-degree angle against the side of the cake (see tip on page 163) and turn the turntable (or your plate) to smooth the sides flat and create a patchy or 'naked' look to the icing on the sides of the cake. (Don't worry if you push some buttercream onto the top of the cake).

To finish the cake with a smooth, 90-degree angle on the top, use a palette knife to neatly drag the top edge of icing into the middle of the cake.

To decorate, mark out a Luminary crescent moon shape on the top of the cake using ground cinnamon, tapering off the ends – this will be your guide for the rest of the toppings. Place chunks of the baked cake crumble at intervals around the crescent shape, with the largest pieces at the widest section of the moon and smaller pieces towards the ends. Repeat with the physalis (with their papery cases torn open like flower petals to reveal the jewel-like fruit inside) and the rosemary sprigs, spacing them evenly and keeping the ends of the moon shape tapered. Finally, sprinkle over the pumpkin seeds and pistachios to fill any gaps.

JESS'
Banoffee Birthday Cake

Jess, one of our interns, is always bubbling with enthusiasm – ready to celebrate even the smallest of life's achievements. She would bake you a cake for practically anything: finishing your book, remembering to walk the dog, making the perfect cup of tea... Her cakes are, in essence, a celebration, so if there ever was the most perfect way to mark another year of *you*, it would be her Banoffee Birthday Cake. The sweet, buttery biscuit base adds a great crunch, which contrasts with the soft banana sponge and velvety salted caramel buttercream – the queen of desserts, in a cake.

SERVES 10–12

For the biscuit base
210g digestive biscuits
    (roughly 14 biscuits)
110g unsalted butter
50g golden syrup

For the banana sponge
375g unsalted butter,
    softened, plus extra
    for greasing
375g self-raising flour, plus
    extra for dusting
375g soft light brown sugar

6 medium eggs
½ tsp ground cinnamon
6 really ripe bananas
    (about 550g)
2 tsp vanilla extract

**For the salted caramel
buttercream**
250g butter, softened
500g icing sugar
200g ready-made caramel
    or dulce de leche (we use
    Carnation Caramel)
1 tsp sea salt flakes

To decorate
¼ tsp ground cinnamon
2–3 digestive biscuits,
    broken into pieces
honeycomb or cinder
    toffee pieces
banana chips
walnuts, hazelnuts or pecans
chocolate chips or buttons
extra ready-made caramel or
    dulce de leche

Preheat the oven to 180°C/160°C fan/Gas Mark 4. Grease and line the base of three 20cm tins with baking paper. Dust the greased edges of the tins with a little flour, tapping out any excess.

Start with the biscuit base. Put the digestive biscuits into a sealable plastic food bag and use a rolling pin to crush them until there are no big chunks of biscuit left.

Gently melt the butter in the microwave or in a small saucepan over a low heat and stir into the biscuit mixture, along with the golden syrup. Mix together until the mixture resembles wet sand and sticks together well.

Tip the biscuit mixture into one of the lined tins and firmly press it down with the back of a spoon to create an even biscuit base – it's really important to form a solid base for the cake, to prevent it crumbling when it comes out of the tin. Place in the fridge for 20 minutes to set firm.

Next, make the banana sponge. In a large bowl, cream the butter and sugar together using a spatula or an electric mixer until it is pale, light and fluffy. Slowly mix in the eggs, one at a time, until fully incorporated, then add the flour and cinnamon and gently fold in using a spatula or spoon.

Mash the bananas using a fork or potato masher and gently mix into the cake batter.

Spoon the batter into the tins, filling them about two-thirds full, and spread them level with a spatula. The tin with the biscuit base should have slightly less mixture in than the other two, so that they're all the same height.

Bake for 25–30 minutes until the sponge is springy to the touch and an inserted skewer comes out clean. Leave in the tins until completely cool.

Meanwhile, make the buttercream. In a large bowl, beat the butter using a spatula or electric mixer until it is slightly lighter in colour. Add the icing sugar, a spoonful at a time, mixing between each addition until it's all incorporated (this will give you a smooth buttercream and avoid too much mess). Stir in the caramel and sea salt and mix to a creamy consistency.

BANOFFEE BIRTHDAY CAKE

When the sponges are completely cool, carefully turn them out of the tins. The biscuit base may break a little at the edges, but don't worry – it should stay bonded to the sponge. Trim the domed tops off the sponges with a bread knife to make them flat.

Place a cake board or serving plate on a turntable or work surface (see tip on page 163) and smear a little buttercream on the top. This buttercream will act as 'glue' and stop the cake from sliding around. Peel off the baking paper from the sponge layers and place the biscuit/sponge layer, sponge-side up, on the cake board or plate. Spread a quarter of the buttercream on the top, pushing it just over the edge.

Place a second sponge layer on top of the buttercream, cut-side down. Spread another quarter of the buttercream on the top of this second layer, pushing it just over the edge.

Place the third sponge layer on top, cut-side down. Spread another quarter of the buttercream on the top of this layer, pushing it just over the edge.

Spread the final quarter of the buttercream around the sides of the cake, until the whole cake is covered in an even layer of buttercream and any gaps are filled. Place a bench scraper at a 90-degree angle against the side of the cake (see tip on page 163) and turn the turntable (or your plate) to smooth the sides flat and create a patchy or 'naked' look to the icing on the sides of the cake. (Don't worry if you push some buttercream onto the top of the cake).

To finish the cake with a smooth, 90-degree angle on the top, use a palette knife to neatly drag the top edge of buttercream into the middle of the cake.

To decorate, mark out a Luminary crescent moon shape on the top of the cake using the ground cinnamon, tapering off the ends – this will be your guide for the rest of the toppings. Place chunks of the the digestive biscuits at intervals around the crescent shape, with the largest pieces at the widest section of the moon and smaller pieces towards the ends. Repeat with the honeycomb pieces and then the banana chips, spacing them evenly and keeping the ends of the moon shape tapered. Use the nuts and chocolate chips to fill in any spaces. Finally, drop or pipe small splodges of caramel into any remaining gaps.

SARAH'S STORY

Sarah came to Luminary after discovering baking as a form of therapy while she struggled with a diagnosis of Post Traumatic Stress Disorder. Her Pistachio, Blackberry and White Chocolate Layer Cake (see page 174) is significant as it was one of the first creations she made when she discovered baking. By the end of the whole process, she was covered in icing sugar and the kitchen was in disarray, but the smiles on her guests' faces as they tucked into slice after slice said it all. That was the moment that changed everything for Sarah and her passion for baking took her on a whole new journey.

As a Luminary graduate, staff member and now business owner (see page 255), Sarah has been unstoppable in sharing her story of recovery and using it as encouragement for others.

'I started baking to help get out of my own head. Even if it was just for five seconds, I finally had a moment of peace... The most important thing someone told me, when I was at the hardest point in my journey, was that "Sometimes we have to break down in order to break through!" My dad was the one who said that to me and I remember thinking, "That's what I'm going to do." It gave me hope that this is not the end – there's hope for me!'

SARAH'S

Pistachio, Blackberry and White Chocolate Layer Cake

Sarah's cake is a delicious way to bring people together, which she can attest to after a neighbour's daughter showed up at her home to learn this sweetly layered recipe. Whether it's broadening your baking horizons or you're savouring each bite of it at a party, this cake suitably weds together the pop of fresh blackberry with the light pistachio sponge, making it perfect for any celebration!

SERVES 10–12

330g unsalted butter,
    softened, plus extra
    for greasing
330g self-raising flour,
    plus extra for dusting
220g caster sugar
6 medium eggs
100ml whole milk
1 tsp vanilla extract
100g unsalted pistachios,
    finely chopped
100g fresh (or frozen)
    blackberries

For the buttercream
150g white chocolate,
    broken into pieces
150g unsalted butter,
    softened
250g icing sugar
½ tsp vanilla extract

To decorate
unsalted pistachios:
    a mixture of whole
    and finely chopped
fresh blackberries: some
    whole, some cut in half
white chocolate buttons
sprigs of fresh rosemary
fresh mint leaves
pomegranate seeds

Preheat the oven to 180°C/160°C fan/Gas Mark 4. Grease and line the base of three 20cm tins with baking paper. Dust the greased edges of the tins with a little flour, tapping out any excess.

In a large bowl, cream the butter and sugar together with an electric mixer until light and fluffy. Mix in the eggs, one at a time, until fully incorporated. Mix in half of the flour, then half of the milk, mixing until no floury or milky patches remain, before adding the remaining flour and milk. Mixing on a low speed, add the vanilla extract and pistachios until incorporated.

Carefully fold the blackberries into the batter by hand, to avoid the mixture turning an unappetising blue-grey colour from the juices they can release.

Divide the batter evenly between the lined tins. Bake for 20–25 minutes until the sponges spring back to the touch and an inserted skewer comes out clean.

Leave to cool in the tins for 10 minutes before gently turning the sponges out onto a wire rack to cool completely.

To make the buttercream, melt the white chocolate by placing it in a bowl set over boiling water (don't let the base of the bowl touch the water). Alternatively, gently melt it in the microwave, being careful to stop and stir it every 30 seconds to avoid burning it.

In a large bowl, beat the butter for 1–2 minutes, then gradually add the icing sugar, a spoonful at a time, mixing it in before adding the next. Once all of the icing sugar is incorporated, mix in the vanilla and melted white chocolate.

When the sponges are completely cool, trim the domed tops off with a bread knife to make them flat.

Place a cake board or serving plate on a turntable or work surface (see tip on page 163) and smear a little buttercream on the top. This buttercream will act as 'glue' and stop the cake from sliding around. Peel off the baking paper from the sponge layers and place the first sponge layer, cut-side up, on the cake board or plate. Spread a quarter of the buttercream on the top of the sponge, pushing it just over the edge.

Place a second sponge layer on top of the buttercream, cut-side down. Spread another quarter of the buttercream on the top of this layer, pushing it just over the edge.

Place the third sponge layer on top, cut-side down. Spread another quarter of the buttercream on the top, pushing it just over the edge.

Spread the final quarter of the buttercream around the sides of the cake, until the whole cake is covered in an even layer of buttercream and any gaps are filled. Place a bench scraper at a 90-degree angle against the side of the cake and turn the turntable (or your plate) to smooth the sides flat and create a patchy or 'naked' look to the icing on the sides of the cake. (Don't worry if you push some buttercream onto the top of the cake).

To finish the cake with a smooth, 90-degree angle on the top, use a palette knife to neatly drag the top edge of buttercream into the middle of the cake.

Decorate the top of the cake with a Luminary crescent moon shape using all of the decoration ingredients. First, sprinkle the finely chopped pistachios into a moon shape, tapering off the ends – this will be your guide for the rest of the toppings. Place the blackberries in the shape, with the whole ones at the widest section of the moon and the smaller pieces towards the ends. Repeat with the whole pistachios and white chocolate buttons. Finish by placing small sprigs of rosemary and mint leaves in among the fruit and use more chocolate buttons and pomegranate seeds to fill in any gaps.

LAURA'S
Lemon and Thyme Drizzle Loaf

Lovely Laura's Lemon Loaf (try saying that a few times!) is a crowd pleaser that will never let you down, much like our lovely baker Laura. Full of zesty lemon and hints of thyme, this springy and jolly cake looks beautiful, drizzled in bright white icing and decorated with delicate sprigs of thyme.

SERVES 8–10

200g unsalted butter,
    softened, plus extra
    for greasing
200g caster sugar
4 medium eggs
a handful of fresh thyme
    (about 10g on the stem),
    leaves picked, plus extra
    sprigs to decorate
200g plain flour
2 tsp baking powder
a pinch of fine salt
finely grated zest of
    2 lemons

For the icing
300g icing sugar
40ml lemon juice

Preheat the oven to 180°C/160°C fan/Gas Mark 4. Grease and line a 900g/2lb loaf tin (23 x 13 x 7cm) with 2 strips of baking paper overlapping on the base of the tin to line each side.

In a large bowl, cream together the butter and sugar for a couple of minutes, until light and fluffy. Add the eggs to the mixture, one at a time, thoroughly beating each one in before adding the next.

In a separate bowl, mix the thyme leaves with the flour, baking powder, salt and lemon zest. Add to the butter mixture and fold in until no floury patches remain.

Spoon the batter into the prepared tin, spreading it level with a spatula. Bake for 40–45 minutes, or until an inserted skewer comes out clean. Leave the cake to cool in the tin for 10 minutes before transferring to a wire rack.

Meanwhile, make a thick icing by mixing together the icing sugar and lemon juice.

While the cake is still warm, poke about 20 holes in the top using a skewer. Gently spoon the icing evenly over the top of the cake, letting it run down the sides in thick ribbons. Decorate with a few fresh thyme sprigs laid over the wet icing. Leave to cool completely so the icing sets before cutting into slices.

Blood Orange Polenta Loaf

We consider a good gluten-free polenta cake a staple in any baker's repertoire, but a worthy alternative to a lemon polenta cake can be hard to come by. Blood oranges are so colourful and have a lovely balance between sweet and sharp – their bright pinky-orange juice livens up the syrup soaked into this cake. Their stunning colouring also gives the baker a fun surprise every time they cut into a fresh orange! If you want to make this cake outside blood orange season, you can substitute regular oranges.

SERVES 8

190g unsalted butter,
    softened, plus extra
    for greasing
190g soft light brown sugar
finely grated zest and juice
    of 2 blood oranges
    (about 150ml)
3 medium eggs
120g polenta/fine cornmeal
    (the finer the better)
200g ground almonds
½ tsp bicarbonate of soda
½ tsp baking powder
a pinch of fine salt
150g natural yoghurt
150g caster sugar

To decorate (optional)
200ml water
150g caster sugar
1 blood orange, cut into
    3–5mm slices

Preheat the oven to 180°C/160°C fan/Gas Mark 4. Grease and line a 900g/2lb loaf tin (23 x 13 x 7cm) with 2 strips of baking paper, arranged in a cross shape overlapping on the base of the tin to line each side.

In a large bowl, use an electric mixer to cream together the softened butter, light brown sugar and orange zest until light, fluffy and paler in colour. Beat in the eggs, one at a time, scraping down the sides with a spatula as necessary, until all the eggs are incorporated (don't worry if it looks as though it has split – once you add the almonds in, it'll come back together).

In a separate bowl, mix together the polenta, ground almonds, bicarbonate of soda, baking powder and salt.

Sift the polenta and almond mixture into the butter mixture and mix until everything is well combined (use an electric mixer on medium speed if you have one), then add the yoghurt and mix until well combined.

Spoon the mixture into the prepared loaf tin and spread flat. Bake for 40–45 minutes until golden brown and a knife or skewer inserted into the centre of the cake comes out clean.

Meanwhile, make the syrup. Combine the orange juice and caster sugar in a small saucepan and bring to the boil, stirring every now and again. Simmer for a further 3 minutes and then remove from the heat and leave to cool in the pan.

Once the cake has finished baking, pierce the loaf about 15–20 times with a skewer, making sure to go right the way through the cake to the bottom of the tin. Pour all of the syrup over the cake and leave to soak in the tin until cooled.

If decorating with candied orange slices, combine the water and sugar in a saucepan over a medium heat and stir and swirl until all the sugar is dissolved and you're left with a translucent syrup. Tip the orange slices into the syrup and bring to the boil, then reduce the heat, cover the pan with a lid and cook on a low simmer for about 40 minutes.

Remove the pan from the heat and leave to cool with the lid on. When cool, take the orange slices out of the syrup and arrange on top of the cake to decorate.

TIP

Syrup soaks best into a cake if either the syrup is hot and the cake cold, or the syrup is cold and the cake hot. In this recipe, we pour cold syrup over a hot cake, but if you need to leave the cake to cool before you can make the syrup, make sure the syrup is steaming hot before pouring it over.

Coffee and Cardamom Cake with Pumpkin-Seed Brittle

Coffee has many good companions: chocolate, caramel, walnuts; but in this cake we think we might just have found our favourite – cardamom. Its spicy warmth complements the coffee's toasty bitterness rather than overshadowing it and allows both flavours to shine together.

SERVES 8–10

165g unsalted butter, softened, plus extra for greasing
165g self-raising flour, plus extra for dusting
135g soft light brown sugar
40g golden syrup
½ tsp vanilla extract
3 medium eggs

seeds from 6 cardamom pods, crushed to a fine powder with a pestle and mortar
½ tsp baking powder
2 tbsp instant coffee granules
2 tbsp boiling water
1 tsp cocoa, for dusting

For the buttercream

75g unsalted butter, softened
150g icing sugar
1 tbsp instant coffee granules
1 tbsp boiling water

For the pumpkin-seed brittle

50g pumpkin seeds
100g granulated sugar

Preheat the oven to 180°C/160°C fan/Gas Mark 4. Grease and line a deep 20cm cake tin with baking paper. Dust the greased edges of the tin with a little flour, tapping out any excess. Additionally, line a baking tray with a sheet of baking paper.

In a large bowl, use an electric mixer to cream together the butter, brown sugar and golden syrup until pale and fluffy. Beat in the vanilla and eggs until well combined (it may separate a little, but don't worry – it'll come back together when you add the flour). Mix the flour, ground cardamom seeds and baking powder into the batter.

In a separate, small bowl, mix together the instant coffee and boiling water, then stir into the batter.

Spoon the batter into the lined tin and smooth out with a spatula. Bake for 30–35 minutes until the sponge springs back to the touch and an inserted skewer comes out clean. Leave to cool in the tin for 5 minutes before tipping out onto a wire rack to cool completely.

To make the buttercream, whisk up the softened butter with an electric mixer and spoon in the icing sugar, a little at a time, until well combined and the mixture is fluffy.

In a separate, small bowl, make a paste with the coffee granules and boiling water and let cool before whipping it into the buttercream.

To make the pumpkin-seed brittle, toast the pumpkin seeds in a dry frying pan over a low heat, shaking the pan now and again, until they've all popped and puffed up. Tip them out in a single layer onto the baking-paper lined tray.

Put the granulated sugar into a small saucepan and let it melt over a medium heat, swirling the pan, but never stirring, until it has turned a copper colour. Pour the caramel over the pumpkin seeds and leave to cool and set hard. This will take 5–10 minutes. When the brittle is set rock hard, snap it into shards.

Ensure the cake is completely cool before starting to decorate. Dollop the buttercream in a mound on top of the sponge and use a palette or butter knife to push it out to the very edges of the cake and create rough waves of icing. Lightly dust the top of the icing with a little cocoa powder and arrange the brittle shards on the top.

PASTRY

Due to pastry's temperament and some pretence around it, our Luminary trainees often find the prospect of making pastry daunting. But with a little guidance and a lot of 'just having a go', it doesn't take them long to realise that it's not as hard as they first thought! It's usually at this moment they also realise how far they've come, how much they've learnt and that, like most things in baking, by faithfully following a recipe, they can create something impressive.

Pastry is flexible by nature, swaying with ease between lusciously sweet and deliciously savoury. It also has many characteristics, from soft and pillowy, to crumbly and short, to flaky and crisp, each variety as wonderful as the next and as varied as the women we train. Our graduates hope that by challenging yourself to make a new pastry, you too will find the same sense of accomplishment and pride as they have.

ANNA'S STORY

Anna* is always our go-to for pastry! With her eye for detail and an Albanian upbringing that meant she mastered the intricate delicacy of pastry from an early age, we're forever grateful to her for introducing us to her impressive Spinach Byrek (recipe on page 192).

Anna made her very first byrek at the age of twelve. After watching her mum make them for years, it was finally her turn. She remembers the challenge of stretching the dough to an exquisitely fine layer and how the scent of white onions filled the whole house. It all came together for the end result of delicious and perfectly flaky byrek.

As the years passed, Anna experienced some painful, life-changing times – and eventually decided to move to the UK for a fresh start. She began to seek out ways to work and support her child, but the doors remained firmly closed. Following a recommendation from a support worker, she discovered Luminary Bakery, and we're so glad that she did!

*Name changed to protect identity

'I wanted to learn, because when I came to this country I didn't know a lot, not even English. But I wanted to change our lives for the better. In life, you meet people who make all the difference. Before I came on the course, I didn't know what I wanted to do. I had two hands and a child to look after, but nothing was happening. Then I met Alice [Luminary's Founder] and she said, "You want something. Let's make it happen together!" That was the motivation I needed. After coming to Luminary, I started to accept that maybe I could do it. And now, I dream!'

ANNA'S*

Spinach Byrek

A customer favourite at our cafés, *byrek* are delicious Albanian flaky pastries stuffed with a savoury filling. Anna's family recipe is at the heart of this version, but with her own added twist: a spinach and feta filling with cracked black pepper on top. The light, savoury flavours sandwiched between layers of buttery pastry are perfect at any time of the day, whether you're hard at work or dreaming up dreams.

MAKES 6–8

For the pastry
300g extra-strong high-protein plain flour, plus extra for dusting (we use Aytac flour or Canadian high-gluten flour)
1 tsp fine salt
220ml warm water
1 tbsp sunflower or vegetable oil
50g ghee, melted, for brushing (see tip)

For the filling
25g ghee
4 tsp sunflower or vegetable oil
300g fresh spinach
300g feta or crumbly sheeps' cheese
salt and cracked black pepper, to taste

*Name changed to protect identity

Start with making the pastry. Mix together the flour and salt in a large bowl, then make a well in the middle and tip in the water and oil. Use a wooden spoon or bench scraper to bring it together into a dough, eventually kneading it together with your hands.

Tip the dough out onto a clean work surface and knead it for 10 minutes until it's really stretchy and elastic. Put the dough back into the bowl, cover with clingfilm or a damp tea towel and leave to rest for 1 hour.

Meanwhile, make the filling. Melt the ghee and oil in a large pan over a medium heat. Add the spinach and gently cook down until wilted and most of the moisture has been cooked off. Remove the pan from the heat and stir in the crumbled cheese. Taste the mixture and season with salt and pepper to taste.

Preheat the oven to 190°C/170°C fan/Gas Mark 5 and grease the base and sides of a 20 x 25cm baking tin with melted ghee.

Lightly flour a clean work surface and rolling pin. Turn the dough out of the bowl and cut it into 6 equal pieces. Taking one piece at a time, roll and stretch each one out as thin as you can using the rolling pin and your hands – the dough should be thin enough to read newspaper print through it. If it starts to stick, lift it up and dust more flour underneath.

Cut the dough into rectangles the same size as your tin (20 x 25cm). Collect any scraps so you can re-roll them and make as many sheets as you can.

Layer a third of the pastry rectangles in the tin, brushing each one with melted ghee before laying the next one on top. Spoon half of the spinach filling on top of the pastry stack and spread it out to make an even layer.

Layer the next third of the pastry rectangles on top of the spinach, again brushing with melted ghee between each layer. Top with the second half of the spinach filling and spread it out flat.

Layer the final third of the pastry on top, brushing melted ghee between each layer as before. Brush the very top layer with the last of the ghee and sprinkle with cracked black pepper.

Bake for 30–35 minutes until deep golden brown on top. Leave to cool, then remove from the tin and cut into 6–8 large squares.

TIP

Ghee is clarified butter and can be found in most large supermarkets, usually in the Asian food section. If you can't find any, then ordinary salted butter will work fine!

Feta, Caramelised Red Onion and Thyme Quiche

In week sixteen of our bakery training programme, we teach our trainees to make shortcrust pastry – and, with it, our infamous quiche. Some have never heard of quiche before; some only have memories of eating soggy beige pastry in church halls; but very few have ever experienced a proper homemade, deep-filled quiche as it should be. Plentiful red onions and feta sit over a crumbly wholemeal pastry, suspended in a silky, just-cooked egg filling. This quiche has gained converts both in and out of our classroom.

SERVES 4–6

For the pastry
150g wholemeal plain flour,
    plus extra for dusting
a pinch of fine salt
75g cold butter, cubed
3 tbsp cold water

For the filling
20g unsalted butter
2 large red onions,
    thinly sliced
1 tbsp soft light brown sugar
1 tbsp balsamic vinegar
4 medium eggs
300ml double cream
50ml whole milk
1 tbsp fresh thyme leaves,
    plus extra for garnish
150g feta cheese
salt and pepper, to taste

First, make the pastry. Combine the flour and salt in a bowl and rub the butter in with your fingertips until it resembles breadcrumbs. Sprinkle over the cold water and bring together into a ball of pastry. If it doesn't come together easily, add a little more water. Wrap the pastry in clingfilm and leave to rest in the fridge for 30 minutes.

To make the filling, melt the butter in a large non-stick frying pan over a medium heat. Add the onions with a pinch of salt and cook for about 20 minutes until soft, stirring occasionally. Stir in the sugar and vinegar and cook over a low heat for 5 minutes until the mixture is sticky. Set aside to cool.

Meanwhile, preheat the oven to 180°C/160°C fan/ Gas Mark 4.

Roll out the chilled pastry on a floured work surface to about 2mm thick, rotating it now and then to avoid sticking. Lift the pastry into a 20cm pie dish, gently lifting and tucking it to line the sides and base of the dish. Leave a little overhang of pastry around the edges.

Line the pastry case with baking paper, fill with baking beans or uncooked rice/lentils and bake for 15–20 minutes. (This weighs the pastry down while it bakes, ensuring it remains flat and even, and is called 'blind baking'.) After this time, remove the beans/rice and the baking paper and return the pastry case to the oven to bake for a further 10 minutes, or until the base feels dry, looks cooked and has no oily patches. Gently trim the excess pastry from around the edge of the tin with a small serrated knife.

Whisk together the eggs, cream, milk, thyme leaves and a good pinch each of salt and pepper.

Fill the base of the pastry case with the sticky onions, crumble the feta over the top, then pour over the creamy egg mixture.

Gently transfer the quiche to the oven and bake for 30–35 minutes until golden brown on the top and there is only a small wobble in the centre.

Sprinkle a few more thyme leaves on top and leave to cool a little before serving warm. Alternatively, cool completely, then refrigerate, before cutting into neat slices.

DOUBRA'S STORY

Doubra's first experience of baking took place after reclaiming a baking book that was due to be thrown away. The methodical process of baking became a stress reliever as she began to create beautiful and luscious treats – starting from simple single-cup bakes and moving on to cakes. This growing enjoyment became a stabiliser during her time living at a London hostel.

With an ambition to grow in her new-found skill and embrace its therapeutic qualities, she kept an eye out for opportunities and eventually was accepted onto Luminary's Employability Training Programme.

Doubra was initially hesitant. Everything was new and the extra effort it took to leave the house and travel across London seemed like a lot of pressure. But, after a while, she became determined to push through!

Even during the bread-making sessions – a class she was not particularly fond of – she motivated herself through all the kneading and frustrations to not only complete the class but graduate from our programme.

'They teach you, even if you feel like you cannot do it or you want to quit. They'll help you see that you're worth more than just letting a little incident ruin things.'

Nigerian Chicken Sausage Rolls

Doubra's sausage rolls pack a punch and will bring instant vibrancy to any picnic basket or packed lunch! The delicious pastry parcels are not only a fusion of Doubra's Nigerian roots and a favourite British classic, but are also testament to her own perseverance. While taking part in Luminary's programme, there were times that she wanted to give up, but her incredible determination meant she always carried on – in the end, she was unstoppable!

MAKES 16

For the rough puff pastry
500g plain flour, plus extra
    for dusting
¼ tsp fine salt
250g cold unsalted butter,
    cut into 1cm cubes

240–270ml cold water
1 medium egg, beaten

For the filling
2 Scotch bonnet or other
    small chillies (use 3 if
    you love spice!)
1 chicken stock cube

30g piece of fresh ginger,
    peeled
6 garlic cloves, peeled
800g chicken sausages,
    casings removed
2 tsp ground nutmeg
1½ tsp cayenne pepper
1 tsp dried thyme

Start with the pastry. Combine the flour, salt and butter in a large bowl and shake to coat the butter in the flour. Add 4 tablespoons of the water at a time, mixing it in with a butter knife to begin with, then using your hands to bring it together into a slightly sticky, butter-dotted dough.

Tip the dough onto a floured work surface and roll out to a large rectangle, 15 x 30cm. With the short sides of the pastry facing you, fold the top short edge down towards you, just past the centre of the dough, then fold the bottom third up over it to make a rectangle a third the size of the original. Rotate the rectangle by 90 degrees and repeat the rolling and folding process another 2 times. Wrap the pastry in clingfilm and chill in the fridge until the filling is ready.

Preheat the oven to 180°C/160°C fan/Gas Mark 4 and line a baking tray with baking paper.

To make the filling, whiz the chillies, stock cube, ginger and garlic in a small food processor to a smooth paste (or cut them up as finely as possible). In a bowl, combine the paste with the chicken sausagemeat, nutmeg, cayenne pepper and dried thyme and mix until well combined.

Cut the chilled pastry in half and place one half back in the fridge. Roll out on a lightly floured surface to a 15 x 50cm rectangle, about 2mm thick. Take half of the filling mixture and arrange in a long log down the middle of the full length of the pastry rectangle. Leave a 2cm gap along one of the long edges. Brush the 2cm strip of pastry with the beaten egg and fold the other long edge of the pastry over the top of the sausage to enclose it. Use a fork to crimp the edges together to form a seal. Cut the roll into 8 pieces and place them on the lined baking tray. Brush the tops with more egg wash and use a sharp knife to score a couple of lines in the top of each one.

Repeat the process with the other half of the pastry and filling mixture to make another 8 sausage rolls.

Bake in the oven for 35–40 minutes until golden brown all over.

Leave to cool for 10 minutes before tucking in, as they'll be piping hot in the middle.

Apple, Sage and Honey Frangipane Tart

Luminary ambassador Benjamina Ebuehi is a wonderful teacher, faithful supporter and inspiration to many of our trainees. Just like an older sister, she has imparted plenty of her recipes, tips and tricks, including how to make her stunning apple pies. We love the way she marries savoury sage with caramelised apples in this tempting tart covered in honeyed frangipane, all neatly contained within her melt-in-the-mouth pastry.

SERVES 8–10

2 Granny Smith apples
a handful of flaked almonds
a drizzle of honey, to serve

For the pastry
275g plain flour, plus extra
    for dusting
100g icing sugar
a pinch of fine salt
160g cold unsalted butter,
    cubed
1 medium egg plus 1 egg
    yolk, beaten together

For the apple and sage sauce
3 Granny Smith apples,
    peeled, cored and
    roughly chopped

2 tsp lemon juice
1 tbsp finely chopped fresh
    sage leaves
1 tbsp caster sugar
3 tbsp water

For the frangipane
225g unsalted butter,
    softened
225g caster sugar
60g honey
1 tsp vanilla extract
3 medium eggs
225g ground almonds
2 tbsp plain flour
a pinch of fine salt

To decorate
10–15 small sage leaves
icing sugar, for dusting

To make the pastry, combine the flour, sugar and salt in a large bowl, add the cold butter and use your fingertips to rub it into the flour until the mixture resembles coarse breadcrumbs.

Make a well in the centre of the flour, pour in the eggs and use a knife to stir and bring the dough together.

Turn the dough out onto a clean work surface and very gently knead it for up to 10 seconds until smooth and soft. Wrap in clingfilm and let it rest in the fridge for 45 minutes.

Unwrap the chilled pastry and place on a lightly floured work surface. Roll the pastry out to about 3mm thick, giving it a quarter turn every so often to avoid it sticking.

Line a 23cm round tart tin (preferably with a loose bottom) with the pastry, letting it overhang the edge of the tin by just over 1cm. Place it in the freezer for 15 minutes to firm up.

Preheat the oven to 200°C/180°C fan/Gas Mark 6.

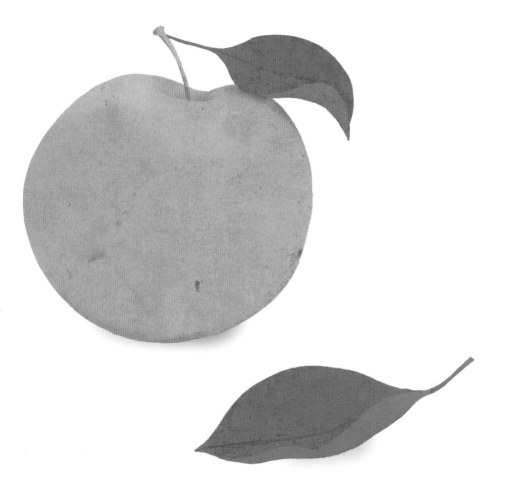

APPLE, SAGE AND HONEY FRANGIPANE TART

To make the apple and sage sauce, put all the ingredients into a small saucepan and cook over a low heat for 12–15 minutes until the apples are softened. Remove from the heat and mash the apples with a fork or potato masher to get a thick sauce. Set aside to cool completely.

To make the frangipane, beat the butter, caster sugar, honey and vanilla together using a stand mixer or electric whisk for 3–5 minutes until pale and creamy. Add the eggs, one at a time, beating well after each addition. Stir in the ground almonds, flour and salt and beat briefly to combine.

Put the frangipane batter into a large disposable piping bag and snip off the end. Set aside.

Remove the pastry from the freezer and use a sharp knife to trim off the overhanging pastry. Spoon the apple sauce evenly over the base of the pastry, then pipe the frangipane on top. Use a palette knife or spatula to smooth out the top.

Core the apples but leave the skins on, cut them into quarters, then thinly slice. Arrange the apple slices on top of the frangipane, letting them overlap slightly. Sprinkle the flaked almonds over the top.

Bake for 45–55 minutes until the pastry is golden and the frangipane is set. If the tart gets too dark before it's completely cooked, cover it with a sheet of foil and continue to bake.

Remove the tart from the oven and leave to cool completely before removing it from the tin. Top with the sage leaves, dust with icing sugar and serve with a drizzle of honey.

Strawberry, Rhubarb and Tarragon Turnovers

Tarragon is a herb that's often banished to savoury dishes, but its unique aniseed flavour makes it the perfect addition to our strawberry and rhubarb turnovers. We love how its bitterness balances the sweetness of our lively strawberry and rhubarb compote in these little handheld pastries.

MAKES 10

For the pastry
250g plain flour, plus extra
   for dusting
⅛ tsp fine salt
1½ tsp caster sugar
125g cold unsalted butter,
   cut into 1cm cubes
8–9 tbsp cold water

For the compote filling
110g strawberries, stems
   removed and sliced
225g rhubarb, cut into
   2cm slices

75g caster sugar
3 tbsp water
1 tsp cornflour
½ tsp finely chopped
   fresh tarragon
1 egg, beaten, to glaze
Demerara sugar,
   for sprinkling

Start with the pastry. Combine the flour, salt, sugar and butter in a large bowl and shake to coat the butter in the flour. Add the water, a couple of tablespoons at a time, mixing it in with a blunt knife to begin with, then bringing it together with your hands to make a slightly sticky, butter-dotted dough. If it's still dry and flaky, add a little more water.

Tip the dough onto a floured work surface and roll out to a large rectangle, 15 x 30cm. With the short sides of the pastry facing you, fold the top short edge down towards you, just past the centre of the dough, then fold the bottom third up over it to make a rectangle a third the size of the original. Rotate the rectangle by 90 degrees and repeat the rolling and folding process another 2 times. Wrap the pastry in clingfilm and chill in the fridge for at least 1 hour.

Meanwhile, make the filling. Combine the strawberries, rhubarb and caster sugar with 1 tablespoon of the water in a medium saucepan over a low heat. Gently cook the fruit for 15 minutes, stirring occasionally, until the juices have been released and it's starting to break down.

Mix the cornflour with the remaining 2 tablespoons of water to make a paste. Pour this into the stewed fruit and mix in well. Continue to cook for 5 minutes, then stir in the chopped tarragon and set aside to cool.

Preheat the oven to 180°C/160°C fan/Gas Mark 4 and line a baking tray with baking paper.

Roll out the pastry on a lightly floured work surface to a 50 x 20cm rectangle, about 2mm thick. Trim the edges of the pastry to make them straight, then cut the pastry into 10 even squares.

Place 1 tablespoon of the fruit compote in the centre of each pastry square, leaving a border clear around the edges. Brush the edges with beaten egg and fold one corner of each pastry over to meet the opposite corner to make a triangle, encasing the compote and sealing the edges.

Transfer the turnovers to the lined tray, brush the tops with more beaten egg and make a small cut in the top of each one to let any steam escape. Sprinkle the tops with Demerara sugar and bake for 30-35 minutes until golden brown.

ABBY'S
Blackberry and Thyme Tart

Abby, a founding baker at Luminary, was inspired by the day her friend and fellow baker Sarah took her out to forage for wild blackberries near our first bakery. Enchanted by the berries' rare appearance, the result was this delicious, colourful tart. As Sarah was vegan and Abby on a refined-sugar- and gluten-free diet, this was something they could both enjoy and a great use for the treasures of their trip.

SERVES 8–10

For the pastry
110g coconut oil
1 tsp finely chopped fresh
    thyme leaves
50g coconut sugar
¼ tsp fine salt
20g ripe banana, mashed
170g gluten-free plain flour

For the blackberry purée
340g fresh blackberries
6 tbsp light maple syrup

For the blackberry filling
250g blackberry purée (see
    above and method)
50g cashew nuts, soaked for
    2–4 hours or overnight in
    cold water, then drained

2 tbsp light maple syrup
a pinch of fine salt
125ml water
½ tsp agar agar powder
    (or 2 tsp vege-gel)
4 tbsp coconut oil

To decorate
170g blackberries
a few sprigs of fresh thyme

To make the pastry, melt the coconut oil in a small pan over a low heat. Once melted, remove from the heat and stir in the chopped thyme. Let the mixture cool and infuse for about 20 minutes.

In a large bowl, whisk together the cool thyme-infused oil with the coconut sugar, salt and banana until the mixture no longer separates. If it won't come together, put it in the fridge and check every 3–5 minutes until it is cool enough to hold together when whisked and looks creamy. Mix in the flour until a dough forms.

Quickly press the dough into the base and sides of a 23cm tart tin (preferably loose-bottomed), focusing on making the edges as even as possible. Poke several holes with a fork over the surface of the pastry, then place in the freezer for 30 minutes.

Meanwhile, preheat the oven to 160°C/140°C fan/Gas Mark 3.

Put the tart tin on a baking tray, line with baking paper and fill with baking beans or uncooked rice/lentils. Bake blind for 10 minutes (see page 195), then remove the paper and beans/rice and bake for a further 15–20 minutes until the base feels dry, looks cooked and has no oily patches.

Transfer the tin to a wire rack and leave to cool completely.

To make the blackberry purée, combine the blackberries and maple syrup in a small saucepan and bring to the boil over a medium heat. Reduce the heat, cover the pan and simmer for 20 minutes. Stir every now and again until the berries have released their juices.

Pour the mixture into a blender or food processor and blend to a vibrant purée, then press through a fine sieve to remove the seeds. Weigh out 250g of the purée and set aside to use in the filling, then chill the remaining purée in the fridge until ready to serve.

To make the filling, put the blackberry purée, soaked and drained cashews, maple syrup and salt into the blender/food processor and process until completely smooth. Leave in the blender while you prepare the agar agar and coconut oil.

In a small saucepan, combine the water with the agar agar and bring to the boil, then continue to boil for another 2–3 minutes, whisking constantly until it dissolves. At the same time, melt the coconut oil in a separate saucepan.

As soon as the agar mixture is ready, with the motor of the blender running, carefully pour the hot agar mixture into the blender, gradually increasing the speed from low to high, then blending at high speed for 30 seconds. Repeat this process with the melted coconut oil, making sure it's fully incorporated before stopping.

Pour the filling into the cooled tart shell. Very carefully, gently tap the tart on the work surface to release any air bubbles. Cut a portion of baking paper large enough to cover the surface of the tart and delicately smooth the paper directly onto the surface of the filling. Chill in the fridge for at least 2 hours.

When chilled, remove the tart from the tin and very slowly peel off the paper, beginning at one side and peeling to the other. Decorate the top of the tart with the blackberries and a few sprigs of thyme and serve with the remaining blackberry purée.

Soda Bread Treacle Tart

At Luminary, we're passionate about soda bread and its inclusivity and versatility (see recipes on pages 66, 68 and 76). It's always best eaten fresh on the day it's baked, but if we do have any left over, we love creating recipes to use it up. This recipe was developed with that in mind, giving soda bread scraps a new lease of life in this sticky, sweet treacle tart.

SERVES 8–10

For the pastry
200g plain flour, plus extra
    for dusting
50g wholemeal plain flour
¼ tsp fine salt
150g cold unsalted butter,
    cubed
1 medium egg, beaten

For the filling
700g golden syrup
finely grated zest of ½ lemon
1½ tbsp lemon juice
2 medium eggs
50ml double cream
¼ tsp fine salt
200g stale soda bread, crusts
    trimmed off

To serve
extra double cream or
    crème fraîche

First, make the pastry. In a large bowl, mix together the flours and salt and tip in the cubed butter. Rub the butter into the flour with your fingertips until it resembles breadcrumbs. Make a well in the middle of the mixture and add the egg, then use a butter knife and then your hands to work it into a ball. Add a little cold water if it's still dry and flaky. Flatten the ball of pastry into a thick disc and wrap in clingfilm. Chill in the fridge for 30–60 minutes.

Roll out the chilled pastry on a lightly floured surface to a circle, about 28–30cm in diameter and 5mm thick. Rotate the pastry and flour the surface as needed, to prevent the pastry sticking.

Gently transfer the pastry to a 20cm round tart tin (about 3.5cm deep and preferably loose-bottomed), gently lifting and tucking it into the edges of the tin to line it all the way around. Use a sharp knife to trim the overhanging pastry in line with the edge of the tin. Place the tin on a baking tray and chill in the fridge for 30 minutes.

Meanwhile, preheat the oven to 180°C/160°C fan/Gas Mark 4.

Line the pastry case with a large piece of baking paper and fill with baking beans or uncooked rice/lentils, right up to the top of the tin. Bake blind for 25 minutes (see page 195), then remove the paper and beans/rice and bake for a further 5 minutes, or until it looks dry with no oily patches and is starting to turn golden.

Meanwhile, make the filling. In a large bowl, whisk together the syrup, zest and lemon juice, eggs, cream and salt until smooth.

Pulse the bread in a food processor or grate on the large holes of a box grater to turn it into breadcrumbs.

Sprinkle the breadcrumbs into the eggy mixture and mix a few times to cover the crumbs in the mixture. Go gently – over-mixing will make a tough, heavy filling.

Once the pastry case is baked, pour in the filling, ensuring it's evenly distributed. Bake for 45–50 minutes until golden brown and the middle is just about set with no wobble.

Cool in the tin for 10 minutes before gently lifting out to serve with double cream or crème fraîche.

Greengage and Elderflower Bakewell Tart

Greengages are a sweet and golden-green variety of plum that make excellent preserves. The sticky jam tastes similar to rhubarb or gooseberry – slightly tart and fruity. It perfectly lends itself to this floral take on a classic, complementing the sweet and mellow elderflower and almonds in the sponge. Divine!

SERVES 8–10

For the pastry
200g plain flour, plus extra
    for dusting
2 tbsp icing sugar
¼ tsp fine salt
100g cold unsalted butter,
    cubed
1 medium egg, beaten

For the frangipane
130g unsalted butter,
    softened
finely grated zest of ½ lemon
100g caster sugar
3 medium eggs
2 tbsp elderflower cordial
150g ground almonds
2 tbsp plain flour

6 tbsp greengage jam
    (see tip)
30g flaked almonds
natural yoghurt, to serve
    (optional)

TIP
Greengage jam is available in most large supermarkets, but if you can't find it try rhubarb, gooseberry or even blackcurrant jam. The tart will be a little different but still delicious!

First, make the pastry. In a large bowl, mix together the flours and salt and tip in the cubed butter. Rub the butter into the flour with your fingertips until you have a mixture like breadcrumbs. Make a well in the middle of the mixture and add the egg, then use a butter knife and then your hands to work it into a ball. Add a little cold water if it's still dry and flaky.

Flatten the ball of pastry into a thick disc and wrap in clingfilm. Chill in the fridge for 30–60 minutes.

Roll out the chilled pastry on a lightly floured surface to a circle, about 28–30cm in diameter and 5mm thick. Rotate the pastry and flour the surface as needed, to prevent the pastry sticking.

Gently transfer the pastry to a 20cm round tart tin (about 3.5cm deep and preferably loose-bottomed), gently lifting and tucking it into the edges of the tin to line it all the way around. Use a sharp knife to trim the overhanging pastry in line with the edge of the tin. Place the tin on a baking tray and chill in the fridge for 30 minutes.

Meanwhile, preheat the oven to 180°C/160°C fan/Gas Mark 4.

Line the pastry case with a large piece of baking paper and fill with baking beans or uncooked rice/lentils, right up to the top of the tin. Bake blind for 20 minutes (see page 195), then remove the paper and beans/rice and bake for a further 5 minutes, or until it looks dry with no oily patches and is starting to turn golden. Transfer the tin to a wire rack and leave to cool completely.

Meanwhile, make the frangipane. Cream together the butter, lemon zest and sugar with an electric mixer on a medium speed until pale and aerated. Beat in the eggs, one at a time, followed by the elderflower cordial. Gently mix in the ground almonds and flour until they're incorporated.

Spread the jam across the base of the cooled pastry case. Dollop the frangipane mixture on top in 5 large blobs and spread flat with a spatula. Sprinkle over the flaked almonds. Bake for 35–40 minutes until the frangipane springs back to the touch when lightly pressed.

Let cool completely, then remove from the tin. Serve with yoghurt, if you like.

Peach and Raspberry Gal-ettes

Our 'gal-ettes' were originally made to celebrate International Women's Day, in honour of all of the 'gal pals' and wonder women in our community and across the globe. These individual free-form tarts are crafted from buttery shortcrust pastry filled with fresh peaches and raspberries. Both sweet and tart, juicy and crumbly, this recipe acts as a reminder that balance is important and celebrates working towards a more gender-balanced world.

MAKES 12

For the pastry

320g plain flour, plus extra
    for dusting
1 tbsp Demerara sugar
½ tsp fine salt
225g frozen unsalted butter
6 tbsp cold water, or more
    as needed

For the filling

4 peaches, halved, stoned
    and cut into 5mm slices
250g raspberries
2 tsp cornflour
2 tsp Demerara sugar, plus
    extra for sprinkling
1 medium egg, beaten,
    to glaze

To make the pastry, mix together the flour, sugar and salt in a large bowl. Use a box grater to grate the frozen butter into the flour and briefly rub it in until the pieces are the size of oats and well coated in the flour. Make a well in the middle of the mixture and add the cold water, using a butter knife or bench scraper to mix it together into a dough. If it's really dry and flaky, mix in an extra 2–3 tablespoons of water. Bring the dough into a disc shape, wrap in clingfilm and place in the fridge to rest for at least 1 hour.

Meanwhile, make the filling. Put the peach slices and raspberries into a bowl and gently toss in the cornflour and sugar to coat the fruit.

Preheat the oven to 200°C/180°C fan/Gas Mark 6. Line a couple of baking trays with baking paper.

Unwrap the chilled pastry and place on a lightly floured work surface. Roll out the dough to 5mm thick. Using a bowl or small plate as a guide, cut out 12cm circles from the pastry and transfer them to the lined baking trays.

Evenly arrange the fruit in the centre of each pastry circle, leaving at least 2.5cm clear around the edges. Fold, pleat and seal the edges of the dough over the edges of the filling, leaving the middles exposed. Brush the edges of the pastry with beaten egg and sprinkle with a little extra sugar.

Reduce the oven temperature to 180°C/160°C fan/Gas Mark 4, then immediately place the gal-ettes into the oven to bake for 30–35 minutes until the pastry is golden brown and the fruit is bubbling.

Leave to cool a little before serving.

DESSERTS

Dessert, pudding, afters, a *sweet*... whatever you call it, we're *those* people – pudding people! We'll take or leave a starter, but for us a meal's not finished until dessert has been served and spoons licked clean. Dessert speaks of hospitality, care and generosity. It prolongs a meal, providing space to savour time together and enjoy conversation and connection. It might be as small as a piece of fruit or a dollop of yoghurt, but if the opportunity arises we love to embrace desserts in all their glory and really make a show of it.

At Luminary, we're also people people – thriving in these moments of gathering and community. We can't think of anything worse than being stuck in the kitchen, slaving over a highly complicated and intricate show stopper while our guests are having fun... without us. For this reason we've pulled together the recipes in this chapter to be delicious, but also straightforward and stress-free, so you can spend precious time with those you love. The perfect ending to a meal!

TANYA'S STORY

Although contentment was a rarity in her childhood home, happy memories of being in the kitchen with her mother have been reassuring to Tanya when life hasn't been so kind.

After a traumatic attack in which Tanya barely escaped with her life, she became more determined than ever to seek restoration for her life. She found this Jamaican recipe (see page 220) among many others to be therapeutic during her recovery. She courageously began to volunteer with charities who were helping other women from domestic violence backgrounds and began exploring business opportunities that would give her independence.

With Tanya's ambition to start her own business growing, she was introduced to Luminary. Over the period of the course and observing the resilience of the other women she met, she was inspired! Tanya was able to draw out the talent and skills that were already rising within herself.

Today, cooking and baking has become a means for Tanya to inspire hope in those who have undergone similar life-changing experiences to her own. Whether it's sharing freshly baked goods or learning how to create them, food has a significant way of bringing people together. Tanya's tip, whether you're new to baking or a true veteran, is:

'Always cook with love.'

'Even before I arrived, I got a sense that Luminary believed in me. They want you to do well! Their way of working inspires you to do well. They give you hope. They really empower women to be their best selves.'

TANYA'S

Banana Fritters with Cinnamon Sugar

The delectability of Tanya's banana fritters leave no room for debate. With their vibrancy rooted in Jamaican culture, your senses are destined to awaken as soon as the oil gets hot! This was one of the first Jamaican recipes Tanya learned and she has fond memories of being in the kitchen with her mother as the irresistible aromas of sweet banana and cinnamon sugar filled the room.

SERVES 4
(MAKES ABOUT 16)

3 medium bananas (about
    330g peeled weight)
⅛ tsp freshly grated nutmeg
½ tsp ground cinnamon
1 tsp vanilla extract
4 tbsp water

40g soft light brown sugar
160g plain flour
½ tsp baking powder
a pinch of fine salt
4 tbsp vegetable or
    sunflower oil, or more
    as needed, for frying

For the cinnamon
sugar
120g caster sugar
1 tsp ground cinnamon

To serve
yoghurt or vanilla ice cream
    (dairy-free, if you like)

In a medium bowl, mash the bananas until they are creamy with just a few small chunks left. Stir in the nutmeg, cinnamon, vanilla, water and light brown sugar until combined. Sift the flour, baking powder and salt over the mixture and mix in until you have a thick batter.

Make the cinnamon sugar by stirring together the caster sugar and cinnamon in a shallow bowl and set nearby.

Heat the oil in a large non-stick frying pan over a medium heat. To test when it's hot enough for frying, add a small dollop of the batter to the oil and watch for it to sizzle and brown. When it's hot enough, carefully drop tablespoons of the banana batter into the pan, swirling the oil over them as they spread out. It's best to fry no more than 5–6 fritters at a time so you don't overcrowd the pan. Fry for 3–4 minutes on each side until the fritters are a dark golden brown. Lift them out of the pan with a slotted spoon and drain on paper towels for 30 seconds.

Add a little more oil to the pan, if needed, and repeat until all the batter is used up.

Tip the still-hot fritters into the cinnamon sugar and turn to coat on every side. Serve immediately, still warm from the pan, with a dollop of yoghurt or a scoop of vanilla ice cream.

Apricot and English Breakfast Tea Clafoutis

We can't think of a lovelier way to round off a dinner party than with our cheery, just-warm, apricot-studded clafoutis. Somewhere between a baked custard and a flan, you're aiming to bake the clafoutis until there's just a little wobble left in the middle and the edges are puffed and golden. It's also ideal for those who like to get ahead. You can make the batter up to a day in advance and leave it in the fridge until you're ready to bake. Just pour the batter into the dish and pop the clafoutis in the oven as you're sitting down to start the meal. It'll be ready as soon as you are!

SERVES 6

320g ripe apricots

70g caster sugar

2 tbsp Cointreau

270ml whole milk

1 English breakfast tea bag

20g unsalted butter, melted,
    plus extra for greasing

40g Demerara sugar

50g plain flour

a pinch of fine salt

2 medium eggs

finely grated zest of
    ½ orange

icing sugar, for dusting

Slice the apricots in half down their creases and twist to remove the stones and separate the halves. Place the halves in a bowl with 30g of the caster sugar and the Cointreau and stir together, bashing the apricots a little with a spoon. Cover the bowl and leave to soften for a minimum of 30 minutes, but ideally for a couple of hours or overnight.

Bring the milk to a simmer in a small saucepan over a medium heat. As soon as it comes to a simmer, turn off the heat and stir in the tea bag and butter until it is melted. Set aside to cool and infuse.

Preheat the oven to 200°C/180°C fan/Gas Mark 6 and grease the base and sides of a 20cm baking dish with a little butter. Tip the Demerara sugar into the greased dish, then shake the dish from side to side to cover the base and sides with a sugary coating.

Add the remaining 40g of caster sugar, the flour and salt to a large bowl and mix together. Make a well in the middle, crack in the eggs and whisk to combine. Strain in the cooled milk mixture, add the orange zest and whisk until there are no lumps remaining.

Arrange the apricot halves in the bottom of the sugared dish.

Pour any remaining apricot juices into the batter mixture and whisk in.

Pour the batter over the apricots and bake for 30–35 minutes until the clafoutis is set to the touch but still has a bit of a 'wobble' in the middle.

Leave to cool for 10 minutes, then dust with icing sugar and serve warm.

SUSIE'S
Cardamom and Orange Butterscotch Pudding

Susie used to work as a baker onboard a ship, which made her a dab hand in the galley-like kitchen in Luminary's second premises. Although she kept us afloat on harder days with her humour and silly stories, we always knew she meant business. This sticky cardamom pudding, smothered in silky orange butterscotch sauce is no exception!

SERVES 8

For the cardamom pudding
110g unsalted butter,
    softened, plus extra
    for greasing
finely grated zest and juice
    of 1 orange
250g dried dates (preferably
    Medjool), pitted
    and chopped
175g soft dark brown or
    muscovado sugar
4 medium eggs
seeds from 10 green
    cardamom pods, crushed
    as finely as possible with
    a pestle and mortar
225g plain flour
1 tsp baking powder
1 tsp bicarbonate of soda

For the orange
butterscotch sauce
100g caster sugar
200ml double cream
60ml freshly squeezed
    orange juice
½ tsp flaky sea salt
150g unsalted butter,
    at room temperature

To serve (optional)
crème fraîche

Preheat the oven to 160°C/140°C fan/Gas Mark 3 and grease and line a 20cm square baking tin with baking paper.

Combine the zest and orange juice along with the dates in a small saucepan and bring to a simmer over a medium-low heat. Continue to simmer for 5–10 minutes until the dates are soft.

Transfer the dates and juice to a food processor and blitz to a smooth paste, then set aside to cool.

Using an electric mixer, cream the butter and brown sugar together until soft, light and fluffy. Crack in the eggs, one at a time, beating between each addition, followed by the cooled date paste and mix until combined. Sift the ground cardamom seeds, flour, baking powder and bicarbonate of soda over the mixture, and fold in until fully incorporated.

Spoon the batter into the lined tin and smooth it over with a spatula. Bake for 30–35 minutes until the sponge springs back to the touch and an inserted skewer comes out clean. Leave to cool in the tin for about 5 minutes.

While the sponge pudding is baking, make the orange butterscotch sauce. Heat the caster sugar in a medium saucepan over a high heat and watch for it to melt. Keep swirling the saucepan (don't stir!) until it's fully melted and starting to turn golden. Wait for the caramel to go a deep amber colour before slowly whisking in the double cream and orange juice. It might splutter a bit to start with – but don't be alarmed, just be careful. Add the salt, then slowly stir in the butter, a little at a time, until it's all mixed in.

Cut the still-warm sponge into large squares and serve smothered in the butterscotch sauce, adding a spoonful of crème fraîche, if you like.

Chocolate Espresso Torte with Ginger Wine Pears

The opulent pairing of chocolate and pears is a classic – but add in coffee, ginger and booze and you're ready for a party! This rich chocolate cake gives a second life to the coffee grounds left over in a cafetière or an espresso machine, and makes the torte all the more dark and delicious. We love serving it alongside these sweet poached pears, tender in texture but with a fiery kick of ginger.

SERVES 8

For the torte
175g unsalted butter, softened, plus extra for greasing
2 tsp cocoa powder, for dusting
200g dark chocolate (70% cocoa solids)
30g leftover coffee grounds (see tip)
125g caster sugar
200g ground almonds
1 tsp vanilla extract
¼ tsp fine salt
4 medium eggs, separated

For the pears
400g caster sugar
600ml ginger wine
1 tsp vanilla extract
2 cinnamon sticks
3 star anise
8 pears, slightly under-ripe, with stalks still intact

For the topping
100g dark chocolate (70% cocoa solids)
60ml double cream

To serve
crème fraîche

Preheat the oven to 150°C/130°C fan/Gas Mark 2. Lightly grease the base and sides of a 25cm springform cake tin with a little butter. Line the base with a circle of baking paper and dust the inside edges of the tin with a little cocoa, tipping out any excess.

Break up the chocolate and place in a heatproof bowl. Melt it in the microwave in short bursts (stirring it regularly to avoid it burning). Alternatively, set the bowl over a pan of boiling water (ensuring the base of the bowl does not touch the water) until it's fully melted. Stir in the coffee grounds and set aside.

Using an electric mixer, cream together the butter and sugar until light and fluffy. Mix in the melted chocolate and coffee mixture, ground almonds, vanilla, salt and egg yolks until well combined.

In a separate, clean bowl use a clean electric whisk to whisk the egg whites until they form stiff peaks when the beaters are lifted sharply out of the bowl. Gently fold the egg whites into the chocolate mixture until no whites remain, trying to retain as much air as possible.

Spoon the batter into the lined tin and smooth it out flat with a spatula. Bake for 35–40 minutes until the torte is firm on the edges but still a little squishy in the middle. Leave it in the tin to cool completely.

Meanwhile, poach the pears. Combine the sugar, ginger wine, vanilla, cinnamon and star anise in a pan large enough that when the pears are added they can be fully submerged in the syrup. Set the pan over a medium heat and bring to the boil, then reduce the heat and simmer for 5 minutes.

TIPS
If you haven't made a pot of coffee or have any used grounds to hand, you can use freshly ground coffee – just reduce the amount to 20g.

If you are only serving 4, the pear recipe can be halved quite easily.

While the syrup is simmering, peel the pears, just removing the skin and keeping the stalks intact. Cut a very small slice off the bottom of each pear so they can stand upright on their bases.

Add the pears to the poaching liquid, bring back to a very gentle simmer and cover with a lid. Cook for 20–30 minutes until tender when tested with an inserted cocktail stick or the point of a knife. Remove from the liquid with a slotted spoon and leave, standing upright, to cool.

To make the topping, chop the chocolate as finely as you can and tip into a bowl. (If you have a food processor, it can make this a bit easier.) Heat the cream and 3 tablespoons of the poaching liquid in a small pan over a medium heat until it starts to bubble. As soon as you see it bubble, immediately remove from the heat and pour the mixture over the chopped chocolate. Leave to stand for 1 minute before mixing it all together with a spatula until the mixture is thick and glossy.

Remove the torte from the tin and transfer it to a serving plate. Pour the topping mixture over the torte and spread it out with a spatula to create an even glaze that just starts to run down the edges.

Serve each slice of torte with a poached pear and a good spoonful of crème fraîche.

TIP

Any leftover poaching syrup can also be refrigerated and used in cocktails – try adding a dash to some prosecco, or a G&T garnished with a slice of pear or lime. For a non-alcoholic cocktail, add 2 tablespoons of the syrup to a glass, top up with soda or tonic water and garnish with a slice of pear or lime and a sprig of rosemary. Alternatively, the poaching liquid can be boiled down to a thick and sticky syrup that is delicious drizzled over ice cream, yoghurt, waffles, pancakes or porridge.

Baked Cheesecake with Roasted Figs

Rachael is one of the unsung 'boss babes' of the bakery, having carried us through some of our biggest challenges and changes. She's been steadfast and always championed others into the limelight. Her baked cheesecake, on the other hand, needs no introduction: gloriously silky and heaped with glistening honey-roasted figs, it'll unashamedly turn all the heads at the table.

SERVES 8–10

For the base
90g unsalted butter, melted, plus extra for greasing
200g digestive biscuits
1 tbsp caster sugar

For the cheesecake filling
900g full-fat cream cheese
3 tbsp plain flour
225g caster sugar
a pinch of fine salt
200ml sour cream
2 tsp vanilla extract
3 large eggs plus 1 yolk
finely grated zest and juice of 1 lemon

For the topping
140g sour cream
1 tbsp caster sugar
a squeeze of lemon juice

To decorate
4 fresh figs
1 tbsp soft light brown sugar
½ tsp ground cinnamon
2 tbsp runny honey
60g shelled pistachios and almonds, roughly chopped

Preheat the oven to 160°C/140°C fan/Gas Mark 3. Grease and line the base of a 23cm round springform cake tin with baking paper.

First, make the base. Put the digestive biscuits into a food processor and blitz to a fine crumb with no large lumps. Alternatively, put them into a sealable freezer bag and bash with a rolling pin.

Melt the butter in a saucepan over a medium heat, then stir in the biscuit crumbs and tablespoon of caster sugar. Once coated in the melted butter, tip the crumbs into the cake tin and press down to create a flat base layer. Bake for 10 minutes, then leave to cool

Increase the oven temperature to 200°C/180°C fan/Gas Mark 6.

Next, make the cheesecake filling. In a large bowl, beat the cream cheese for 2–3 minutes until loosened, then gradually beat in the flour, caster sugar and salt. Add the sour cream, vanilla extract, eggs and egg yolk, lemon zest and juice, and mix until smooth and uniform in consistency.

Grease the inside edge of the cake tin with a little more butter and pour the filling on top of the biscuit base, smoothing it out with a spatula if it's not level. Bake for 15 minutes, then reduce the oven temperature to 90°C/60°C fan/Gas Mark ½ and bake for a further 50 minutes until the cheesecake is firm around the edges with a little wobble in the middle. Turn off the oven and open the door, but leave the cheesecake in the oven for another 2 hours, to slowly cool down as the oven cools.

To make the topping, whisk together the sour cream with the caster sugar and lemon juice. Once the cheesecake has cooled, spread the mixture over the top and transfer to the fridge to set for up to 8 hours or overnight.

At least 1 hour before serving, roast the figs. Preheat the oven to 180°C/160°C fan/Gas Mark 4 and slice each fig into quarters. Put the figs into a small roasting tin, sprinkle over the brown sugar and cinnamon and bake for 15–20 minutes until softened and browned. Leave to cool for 15 minutes before drizzling over the honey.

Meanwhile, tip the chopped nuts onto a baking tray and toast in the oven for 10 minutes until fragrant.

To serve, remove the cheesecake from the springform tin and transfer to a large plate. Place the roasted figs on top, drizzle with any remaining honey syrup from the figs and sprinkle with the toasted nuts.

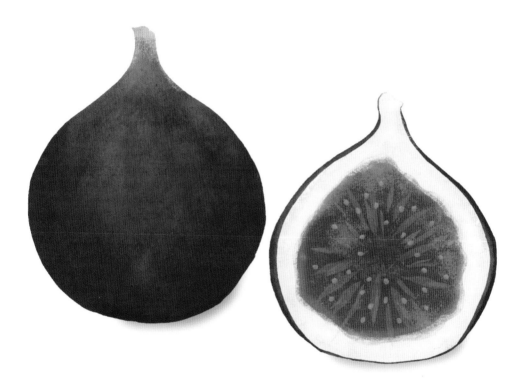

TIP

If you want to make this recipe gluten free, substitute the digestive biscuits for gluten-free biscuits and use gluten-free plain flour instead of regular plain flour.

Cinnamon-Swirl Bread-and-Butter Pudding

If you made our Cinnamon Swirls from earlier in the book (see page 52) and haven't managed to eat them all while they're still fresh (practically impossible in our bakeries), this recipe will transform your leftover buns into a wonderful, comforting, custard-y dessert.

SERVES 6–8

20g unsalted butter, softened, for greasing
4 large, stale cinnamon buns (about 600g)
50g raisins or sultanas (chocolate chips are also delicious if you're not a fan of dried fruit)
4 medium eggs
25g soft dark brown sugar
1½ tbsp dark rum
200ml double cream
600ml whole milk
2 tsp ground cinnamon
¼ tsp fine salt
2 tbsp Demerara sugar

Lightly grease a 30 x 25cm pie dish with butter.

Cut the stale cinnamon buns into vertical slices, 1–2cm thick. Arrange the slices, standing up and overlapping one another in the dish. Sprinkle over the raisins, allowing some to drop in between the bun slices.

Whisk together the eggs, dark brown sugar, rum, cream, milk, cinnamon and salt. Pour the mixture over the bun pieces and leave to stand for 30 minutes, so the bread can soak up the custard.

Meanwhile, preheat the oven to 170°C/140°C fan/ Gas Mark 3.

Sprinkle the Demerara sugar over the top of the pudding.

Bake for 40–45 minutes until it has puffed up and has a very slight wobble in the middle.

Leave to stand for 5 minutes before serving warm.

KATIE'S
Buttermilk Panna Cotta with Grapefruit Caramel

Utterly charming, just like Katie, these creamy panna cotta topped with glowing grapefruit caramel really are quite the picture. Katie's use of buttermilk is inspired by her Irish upbringing and, when made in small glasses with their distinct layers on show, no one can resist taking a spoon to their smooth and light cream.

MAKES 6–8

For the panna cotta
3 sheets of leaf gelatine
350ml buttermilk
    (or 300g full-fat yoghurt
    and 50ml whole milk)
250ml double cream
50g caster sugar
½ vanilla pod, sliced
    lengthways and seeds
    scraped out

For the caramel
50g caster sugar
2½ tbsp water
120ml fresh red
    grapefruit juice
1 tbsp salted butter

To serve
1 red grapefruit

For the panna cotta, first soak the gelatine leaves in a small bowl of cold water. Place 250ml of the buttermilk (or the 300g yoghurt, if using) in a large heatproof bowl, along with the double cream and set aside.

Place the remaining 100ml of the buttermilk (or the whole milk, if using), the sugar and the seeds from the vanilla pod in a small saucepan and bring to the boil.

Take the pan off the boil, squeeze any water out of the gelatine leaves and add the gelatine to the pan, stirring until it is completely dissolved. Strain the mixture through a sieve into the bowl with the buttermilk and cream and stir until thoroughly combined.

Pour the mixture between 6–8 small serving glasses or ramekins (depending on their size), leaving about 2cm clear at the top. Place in the fridge to set for a minimum of 3 hours.

To make the caramel, put the sugar and water into a small saucepan and bring to the boil over a medium heat. Cook until it becomes a dark amber colour, then slowly add the grapefruit juice, a little at a time. Be careful – it will spit and spurt and the caramel will set hard in the pan. Bring the caramel back to the boil and simmer for about 5 minutes until the hardened sugar dissolves and it has reduced to a thicker, pourable sauce. Remove from the heat and stir in the butter, a little at a time, until it's all incorporated.

Transfer the warm caramel to a jug and leave at room temperature until the panna cotta are set.

To serve, slice the top and bottom off the grapefruit and, using even downward strokes, slice the skin off the grapefruit, making sure to remove any white pith. Cut in between the membranes to obtain whole segments. Squeeze any remaining grapefruit juice back over the segments. Spoon the caramel over the top of each panna cotta and place 1–2 grapefruit segments on top to decorate. Serve immediately.

RACHEL'S
Blueberry and Basil Pavlova

If you were to walk into our kitchen on week 21 of our training programme, you would be met by a gaggle of trainees, excitedly huddled around mixers, in awe of what they'd just made for the first time: meringue. Thick and glossy, bright white peaks, whisked up from only a few egg whites and sugar – the wonder and thrill of it never gets old. Once the meringue is out of the oven and piled high with cream and fruit, our trainees' pride in their centrepiece creations quickly leads you to being handed platefuls of pavlova to try. This recipe is a favourite of Rachel, our bakery trainer and former Head Baker. We hope the enchanting combination of blueberries and basil in her compote fills your kitchen with the same wonder and joy as ours.

SERVES 8–10

For the meringue
3 medium egg whites
finely grated zest of ½ lime
    plus 2 tsp lime juice
a pinch of fine salt
200g caster sugar
1 tsp cornflour

For the blueberry and
basil compote
400g frozen blueberries
    (fresh are nice too)
75g caster sugar
2 tsp lime juice
3 tsp cornflour
2 tbsp cold water
6 large basil leaves,
    finely chopped

To serve
300ml double cream
a handful of basil leaves
finely grated zest of ½ lime

TIPS
Make sure all the equipment you need is spotlessly clean and grease free.

A pavlova is best when baked and left to cool in the oven, the residual heat finishing the cooking. You can leave the oven door slightly ajar, if you wish, to avoid moisture build-up and help it dry out completely. We always bake the meringue the night before we want to serve it and leave it to cool as we sleep. All that's left to do on the day is to whip up some cream and compote and decorate your pavlova.

Preheat the oven to 180°C/160°C fan/Gas Mark 4 and line a baking tray with baking paper.

In a large clean bowl, use an electric whisk to whisk the egg whites, lime juice and salt until they form stiff peaks when the beaters are lifted sharply out of the bowl. Whisk in the sugar, adding a third of it at a time and whisking for a couple of minutes between each addition. Once the meringue is really thick, whisk in the cornflour. Finally, add the lime zest and gently fold it in.

Spoon the meringue into a heap on the lined baking tray and gently spread to form an even 20cm circle. Use your artistic freedom to make 'waves' and small peaks in the meringue as you wish.

Place in the oven and immediately reduce the temperature to 150°C/130°C fan/Gas Mark 2. Bake for 1 hour until the outside is crisp, then turn the oven off and leave in the oven to cool completely (see tip).

To make the compote, tip the blueberries, sugar and lime juice into a saucepan and leave to defrost over a low heat for about 10 minutes, stirring every now and again. Turn the heat up to medium and cook down for about 10 minutes until some of the blueberries have burst.

In a small cup or bowl, stir the cornflour together with the water to a smooth paste. Add the paste to the blueberry pan and stir to thicken and cook for a few minutes. Stir in the finely chopped basil, then remove from the heat and allow to cool completely – the compote will thicken further as it cools.

When the compote is completely cool, whip the double cream into soft peaks using an electric whisk – it's best to whip until the cream is almost thick and then stop and do the last bit by hand to avoid over-whipping and ending up with 'crumbly' whipped cream. Take a large spoonful of the compote and gently fold it through the cream to ripple it with purple swirls.

Dollop the cream into a big pile in the centre of the meringue and spread out almost to the edge. Spoon the remaining compote on top of the cream and spread it out, leaving some of the cream visible at the edge. Finish with a sprinkling of basil leaves and the lime zest.

Amaretti Meringue Nests with Cherry Compote

For Erin

Grace originally came up with this stunning dessert after receiving an invitation to a dinner party. As someone who felt isolated from everyday relationships, Grace wanted to impress! Suffice to say, her crunchy amaretti biscuit meringues filled with fresh cherry compote with its vivid pink colouring were a culinary game-changer. Not only did Grace's new friends enjoy her dessert, but it helped her find the courage to take a chance on life again. Grace decided to dedicate this recipe to Erin Pizzey* – a driving force for safety and friendship, opening up doors to people who are isolated. 'She set a precedent that coincides with my journey. Without her, people like me may not have been helped!'

MAKES 6

For the meringue
75g egg whites
    (from about 2 eggs)
¼ tsp almond extract
150g caster sugar
6 crunchy amaretti biscuits,
    such as Amaretti di
    Saronno (80g), plus
    an extra 2 biscuits to
    decorate (see tip)

For the compote
150g frozen cherries
30g caster sugar
2 tbsp lemon juice

For the mascarpone cream
100g mascarpone cheese
50ml double cream
25g icing sugar, sifted
1 tsp vanilla extract

TIP
If you're making this as a gluten-free dessert, ensure you buy a brand of amaretti biscuits that doesn't contain wheat.

*Erin Pizzey started the first domestic violence shelter in the modern world, in 1971.

Preheat the oven to 100°C/80°C fan/Gas Mark ½ and line a baking tray with baking paper.

In a spotlessly clean bowl, whisk the egg whites, using an electric mixer on a medium speed, until they have doubled in size and form stiff peaks when the whisk is lifted sharply out of the bowl. Turn the whisk to a higher speed and add the almond extract, then add the caster sugar, a spoonful at a time, until the mixture is glossy and you can't feel any grains of sugar when it is rubbed between your fingers.

Crumble 6 of the amaretti biscuits into 6 separate circles on the baking tray. Carefully pipe or spoon the meringue mixture onto each biscuit mound in a nest shape, making a dimple in the middle. Try to keep the biscuit crumbs on the base of the meringue.

Bake the meringues in the oven for 2 hours, or until they lift off the baking paper easily but before they have browned.

Meanwhile, make the compote. Place the cherries, caster sugar and lemon juice in a saucepan over a low-medium heat and cook for 20–25 minutes, stirring occasionally, until the cherries have cooked down. Set aside to cool.

To make the mascarpone cream, simply place the mascarpone in a bowl and beat it briefly to loosen. Add the double cream, icing sugar and vanilla, and whisk together until the mixture forms soft peaks – be careful not to over-mix or it will become grainy.

Once the meringues and compote are cool and you are ready to serve, top each nest with some of the mascarpone cream, followed by a large spoonful of compote, letting it drip down the sides. Crumble over the remaining amaretti biscuits and serve immediately (they will go soggy if you do this in advance).

INDEX

SPECIAL INDEXES

GLUTEN-FREE RECIPES

LACTOSE-FREE RECIPES

VEGAN RECIPES

30 MINUTES OR LESS RECIPES

ECONOMICAL RECIPES

ACKNOWLEDGEMENTS

When it comes to thanking our ever-supportive and passionate community, the list could literally go on and on. Our journey has connected us with people who've travelled hundreds of miles to help us renovate, paint and maintain our buildings; who have willingly volunteered to wash an endless array of pots; who have been inspired to paint, draw and photograph our baked goods; who have used their influence to shed light on the work we do; who have sent encouraging words right when we needed them; and who donated clothes, food and gifts for our wonderful women. You have helped us get to where we are and we thank you all deeply!

Firstly, thank you to the Kahaila community. This is where the idea for Luminary came about and we are so grateful to every single one of you who has journeyed with us through volunteering, continually praying for and championing this endeavour.

To Good Shepherd Mission Bethnal Green, our first home as a bakery. We thank you for taking a chance on us and believing in our vision. You not only made each and every one of us feel welcomed into your community, but you also supported our grassroots.

To Husk Coffee & Creative Space, thank you for being our home-in-transition. So many beautiful stories, memories and adventures happened in your tiny kitchen and classroom. Thank you for making room for us to completely take over your cooking space when we needed to ramp up to full-time training and baking.

To all our dedicated stockists and customers, thank you for being the engine behind Luminary. For enabling us to employ more women who need a second chance.

Thank you to Ben & Jerry's and Food Innovation Solutions for taking a risk on us and partnering with our little social enterprise. You taught us so much about what it means to create such wonderful products.

Thank you to all our investors, donors and financial supporters, for joining us on this exciting journey and for taking a chance on what we are doing. None of what we do could happen without you! Thank you for being there for us at whatever point you joined along the journey and for having faith in our desire to bring change.

Thank you to our selfless volunteers, mentors and ambassadors, past and present, for being the heart and soul of Luminary. You went above and beyond to make us what we are today... and helped us have so much fun along the way! A particular thank you to Rachel Joy Price, the creator of our iconic logo, for taking the time to form such a symbol of hope.

To our trustees and directors, you've brought in the support, wisdom and guidance that we truly needed. Thank you for giving up your time, energy and brains to steer this ship.

To the Duchess of Sussex and her wonderful team, thank you for sharing the work we are doing with the world, for taking the time to get to know us and for championing our women so powerfully.

To Kate and her incredible team at HQ, to our creative copy editor, Emily, and to our clever designer, Georgie, thank you for your passionate care for our Luminary women and desire to do something so unique with this book. We are so grateful that you believed in us, encouraged us and helped make it the best it could be.

To our talented illustrator, Carrie, thank you for working with us and introducing us to the beautiful world of watercolour. We are grateful for your dedication to helping bring our recipes to life.

To our dedicated literary agent, Charlotte, thank you for seeing something special in your local bakery. Others have asked us to create a book, but we felt so safe in your hands – thank you for everything you have done to make this a reality.

To all our fearless recipe testers around the world, thank you for your late-night escapades! All of the time and energy you put into making sure our recipes were delicious has been so valuable.

To the women who shared their stories in this book, thank you for opening up part of your life to us and the world. Your hope, transformation and perseverance continue to inspire us all every day.

To all our trainees, past and present, thank you for being a part of our family and making it the fun, generous, supportive, empowering, diverse, beautiful thing that it is today!

To our devoted friends and family, thank you for being as much a part of the journey as everyone else. You have often been in the background, cheering us on, offering a listening ear, and giving us the energy we needed to keep going. You have been crucial in helping us continue to tackle barriers and grow our vision. Thank you for having our backs! And thank you again to all our recipe creators and contributors – your journey with us on this cookbook adventure has been a joy.

We are honored to have such a loyal community! We have seen ups and downs throughout the years as a social enterprise, but have risen above it more hopeful than before because of your devotion and faith in empowering all women. Together we have made, are making, and will continue to make a difference.

With love,
Your Luminary Family

ABOUT LUMINARY

Luminary Bakery is a social enterprise supporting some of the UK's most disadvantaged women to thrive, through training, employment and community.

This book includes contributions from many of the women in the Luminary community, carefully curated and written by our Head Bakery Trainer **Rachel Stonehouse**. Rachel has worked closely with each contributor to ensure these recipes are delicious, creative and easy for you to bake at home. Additional recipes are Luminary classics, and some she has created exclusively for this book. Rachel has been with Luminary since (almost) day one, moving to London in 2014 to join our fledgling bakery. She later took on the role of our Head Baker and now spends her days in Luminary's kitchen classroom, passing her baking skills on to the trainees on our Employability training programmes.

Woven throughout this book are true stories from some of our incredible graduates, collated and written by our Communications Officer, **Kaila H. Johnson**. Kaila had the honor of spending time interviewing these remarkable women and hearing the narratives and inspirations behind each of their recipe contributions. Having been a cheerleader of Luminary Bakery from day one, Kaila has often been seen operating behind the scenes, helping fill the different positions that a budding charity and business need filling. She now spends her days writing and sharing with the world the stories of rising hope and the noticeable impact taking place at and through Luminary Bakery.

Alice Williams, founder of Luminary, wrote the introduction to *Rising Hope* and has worked closely with the writing team. Alice has led Luminary from the seed of an idea to the thriving multi-site bakery it is today, with a dream of there being a Luminary Bakery wherever it is needed in the UK.

Rachael Coulson, Luminary's Commercial Director, has focused on the flow and composition of *Rising Hope*, shaping and guiding its content to honestly reflect the true essence of Luminary and to captivate our readers with all the insight you would hope to gain from the first ever Luminary cookbook. Rachael joined Luminary three years ago, coming straight from the commercial world with a burning desire to use business as a force for change; she is excited to see how *Rising Hope* inspires others to enter the exciting and transformative world of social enterprise!

RESOURCES

Luminary's social enterprise bakery is made up of talented bakers, baristas and support workers offering opportunities for women to build a future for themselves. We provide a safe and professional environment, empowering women to build their careers through two years of training, community and holistic support. During our 6-month Employability Training Programme, we train groups of women covering baking skills to a professional standard, Level 2 Food Hygiene and character development. Women also are given the opportunity to do work experience within Luminary's cafés and bakery production units. Following the training programme and graduation, our women enter the 18-month Progression Support Programme. They work one-to-one with our progression workers, have the opportunity to apply for paid work at Luminary or external employment opportunities, are linked up with a professional mentor to help reach their goals, offered regular wellbeing workshops, and have access to ongoing practical support and signposting.

If you'd like to know more about Luminary Bakery, head to our website: **luminarybakery.com**

If you or somebody you know are affected by the issues raised in this book, you can find further information and resources at: **luminarybakery.com/resources**

Below are details for the enterprises started by our training programme graduates, referenced in their stories:

Haliberry Cakes and Catering: haliberrycatering.co.uk

Bake Yourself Better: bakeyourselfbetter.com

Strength of a Woman: @strengthofawoman2019

HQ

An imprint of HarperCollins*Publishers* Ltd

1 London Bridge Street

London SE1 9GF

10 9 8 7 6 5 4 3 2 1

First published in Great Britain by HQ

An imprint of HarperCollins*Publishers* Ltd 2020

ISBN: 9780008358327

Design: Georgina Hewitt

Project Editor: Emily Preece-Morrison

Commissioning Editor: Charlotte Mursell

Editorial Director: Kate Fox

Printed and bound in Italy